Rabbiting

RABBITING

BOB SMITHSON

The Crowood Press

First published in 1988 by
The Crowood Press
Ramsbury, Marlborough,
Wiltshire SN8 2HE

British Library Cataloguing in Publication Data

Smithson, Bob
Rabbiting
1. Rabbit-hunting   I. Title
799.2'59322   SK341.R2

ISBN 1 85223 053 3

Picture Credits

Photographs by Peter Collins
Line drawings by John Paley

Typeset by John Weallans Book Production Services
Printed in Great Britain by Biddles Ltd, Guildford

Contents

Introduction

Bob Smithson's credentials for writing this book are immaculate. He is a countryman of the widest possible experience and a man of great perception, with the ability to see what so many of us overlook. He retired in 1983 having achieved a very high standard of proficiency in most of the sporting aspects of country life.

At 19 he killed 10,600 rabbits in a single year, working virtually single-handed, his only allies being a team of ten ferrets and two lurchers. He did not use a gun. His rabbit-killing methods were snaring, trapping, ferreting and using his running dogs. In addition, long-netting both by day and by night produced substantial totals. In more recent times he added night shooting with a rifle to his talents, topping 100 on a number of occasions.

In that first year he worked 5,000 acres, without motorised transport, getting himself and his equipment from place to place with a trade bike – a bicycle equipped with carrying baskets to contain his traps, snares, ferrets, all his other equipment and, of course, the rabbits he caught. He was often obliged to make two and three journeys back and forth, and the sheer graft of this work made it absolutely vital to discover the quickest and easiest route to travel and how to be efficient at killing and conveying rabbits.

At that time Bob's wage was about 7½ per cent higher than that of the farm labourers, and he also received a small bonus for every dozen rabbits he killed. The additional bonus for the estate on which he worked came with his spring and summer kill of stoats, weasels and other vermin that intruded into devices intended to kill rabbits. He worked twelve dozen gin traps (now illegal) and the same number of snares daily, moving four dozen to a new site every 24 hours so that the 5,000 acres were systematically combed for rabbits.

In 1946 after serving in the Army, Bob became a gamekeeper

7

for the How Hill Estate, at Ludham, Norfolk, where some of his achievements set standards difficult to equal. One morning flight produced a total bag of 303 ducks – including 185 teal and many mallard, but in all nine different species to four guns. Nearby marshes were the setting for one of the biggest and most success-ful day's snipe shooting of all time. A marsh became flooded when a pump broke down during a sudden thaw, the snipe revelled in the muddy terrain and six guns killed 116 in a day.

How Hill's 256 acres of arable land yielded a one-day total of 148 brace of partridge and with the long-nets Bob had a top score of 94 rabbits from a single setting of the nets. At a time when it is widely reckoned that a return of 50 per cent is par for the course, Bob Smithson never failed to get a kill of 70 per cent of all the pheasants he had reared.

A pike angler of ability, Bob has caught four pike each weighing 20lb (9kg) or more in one day's fishing and his biggest ever pike to his favourite method, deadbait spinning, weighed 27lb (12.25kg). He became an eel-catcher of distinction, with a

Bob Smithson

biggest single haul of one ton of eels taken from Heigham Sound in twelve worked nets in tandem that he had made himself. Bob made and repaired all his eel nets, made and repaired both purse and long-nets and also made all the snares he has ever used.

The How Hill Estate was sold to the Norfolk County Council in the early 1960s and Bob's role changed. Instead of gamekeeper he became a teacher of environmental studies – ornithology and botany among them. He became responsible for marsh management in the one area where swallowtail butterflies still exist in good numbers at How Hill and taught youngsters and adults alike the ability to see and recognise a variety of birds, from the hen and marsh harrier to the smaller willow warbler and all the finches. He kept the mole and rabbit populations under control in the interests of the lawns and gardens.

He is a popular and engaging speaker at numerous Gun Club and similar functions, illustrating his talks with a wide variety of colour slides covering the shooting and countryside spectrum.

Bob maintains his lifelong interest in the whole sporting scene, remains a picker-up on local estates in the shooting season and continues to be a keen and enthusiastic shot. He continues his dedication to do-it-yourself on the basis that if you know what you are doing and can do it well you can make a product that cannot be beaten.

He considers that the changes he has seen in his lifetime have been so enormous they can never be equalled in any lifespan – from horse and cart to space travel – but he wonders if any of us have truly done enough to ensure the long-term survival of all the things we rate so highly.

Peter Collins

1

Know Your Rabbit

There are two main views of the rabbit. It is a cuddly pet, an animal to be loved and treasured by children, or it is a real pain in the neck – for Britain's farming community. It eats into their profits and for many of them the only good rabbit is a dead one.

There is the middle view – that of the sportsman. He holds the rabbit in high regard as a sporting quarry. He happily helps the farmer but also has some sympathy with the cuddly pet view, if only to the extent that he wouldn't want to be responsible for wiping rabbits out – as if he could! The sportsman thoroughly disapproves of myxomatosis – the plague that now hits rabbit stocks almost annually – and he fervently hopes that reasonable stocks will survive in perpetuity not only for the maintenance of his sport but also out of regard for the rabbit itself.

Rabbits were introduced to this country from France in the twelfth century. At that time the sporting aspect was limited to the use of 'long dogs', the name given in bygone years to the dogs used for coursing – lurchers, etc. The rabbits were introduced in furtherance of sport and for their food value by the landowners of the time. Rabbits were rigorously protected for hundreds of years and soon spread far and wide to become the most familiar wild animal of the British mainland. Their protection was, at least for a time, so stringent that significant numbers of poachers were exiled to the colonies.

It wasn't until 1880 with the passing of the Ground Game Act, giving tenant farmers protection against their landlords and giving them the right to kill hares and rabbits, that the laws were even modestly relaxed. When rabbits were first released in this country they were freed into man-made warrens – artificial holes covered over with a pyramid of cordwood which in turn was covered with faggots. Even very much more recently rabbit populations were encouraged in this way, for I recall being involved in work of this kind at Alfreton Park, Derbyshire, in

1934 – this because the sportsmen of that time and locality wanted to bolt and shoot rabbits for sport.

At that time the burrow entrances were started with lengths of pipe, covered with cordwood and faggots and spaced some 40 yards (36.5 metres) apart in parkland. The wood was loosely stacked to provide the rabbits with temporary cover until such time as they enlarged the burrows themselves. The distance between each man-inspired burrow was just sufficient to give adequate time and space to allow shooting in comfort as the rabbits were bolted. There was a ready market for the rabbits in the local mining community. Some 10 per cent of all these rabbits were black and it is not, of course, unusual to find black rabbits in various parts of the country.

So the sportsman takes the view that the rabbit is a worthy member of the wildlife community, while accepting that most farmers, perfectly understandably, take another view. It falls relatively easy prey to a large number of its predators – man, foxes, stoats, weasels, mink, buzzards and others – yet it is able to maintain itself in very significant numbers and those very numbers do, in fact, shield other important members of the British wildlife community from a high degree of predation.

Foxes, stoats, weasels and other predators are all happy to get a proportion of their diet off the rabbit population and this is a very great protection for our stocks of game birds – pheasants, partridges and grouse – and indeed most other bird species. While the rabbit bears the brunt of the predatory offensive other animals and birds receive the benefit.

The rabbit is widely known as an inoffensive creature. That furthers its cuddly image and it is offensive to no other mammal. That is not to say it isn't perfectly able to compete with its own kind, often aggressively, and in fact at times rabbits inflict serious injury to one another. This especially applies to the old bucks, which have been known to kill off the younger bucks, their main rivals, for obvious reasons.

In recognition of the fact that the rabbit is so inoffensive and far from able to defend itself, nature has applied the customary protection for the species. As the result an adult doe, adult at only six months old, produces a litter within four weeks of conception and the reproductive process begins again within three days of her giving birth. A young doe can, in fact, conceive her first litter at only four months, while a doe of breeding maturity in February can be expected to produce four or even five litters before the autumn.

Litters usually contain anything from two to eight young. The first litter of the year, rabbits born in February, will have themselves reproduced by the autumn so the rabbit has, in fact, a quite awesome reproductive ability. Odd litters can be born at any time of the year, weather controlling the conditioning of the does. Rabbits do not breed communally. They have their individual nests and both does and bucks are promiscuous. There is no permanent relationship.

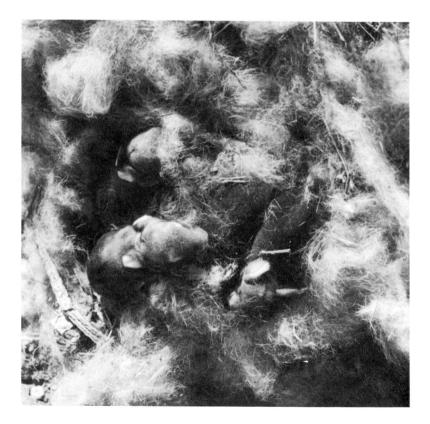

Young rabbits within the nest made from rabbit's hair. These are some nine days old.

Sometimes a doe will extend a dead end within a burrow and construct her breeding chamber; more usually she makes a small hole either out in open terrain or sometimes in a hedgerow. This is known as a 'stop'. Some hedgerow stops are often the beginnings of a new burrow system once the doe and her young move out. I have never known a situation where a doe has used the same breeding stop twice. The stop is a small burrow with only a single entrance. It usually extends no more than 4 to 5 feet (1.2 to 1.5 metres) in length and has an enlarged breeding chamber at its far end. Into this the doe carries dry grass, straw, and suchlike, lining her nest with fur from the belly of her own body. Her young are born in the nest and she leaves them there, protecting them from predators by blocking the hole with soil, which she packs down quite tightly.

She will then go off to her own burrow or will lie rough in ground vegetation until reopening the stop for feeding purposes. She continues this process until the young rabbits, born blind and hairless, have grown fur and are in need of food she cannot supply. So she moves them to a nearby burrow when they are approximately four weeks old and at that time they will have become virtually self-supporting. Thereafter they fend for themselves and she is quickly into preparation for her next litter. I estimate that no more than 50 per cent of all young rabbits survive long enough to reach maturity.

The rabbit's breeding chamber is some 4 or 5 feet (1·25 − 1·5 metres) long and the young are born in a nest of hair where they stay for a month. The doe visits periodically to feed them, opening and closing the entrance on each occasion.

13

Rabbits' nests are the breeding ground of the rabbit flea. The fleas' eggs are laid in the nest and once hatched the fleas feed off the young rabbits. All rabbits carry fleas and it is most significant that does, as the result of being in recent contact with a nest, always appear to have the greatest infestations.

Just as rabbits were imported from France, so too came the modern rabbit plague – myxomatosis. It reached Britain in 1953 in extremely virulent form and in its first major spread was estimated to have killed 60 million rabbits – more than the entire human population of Great Britain.

Myxomatosis first shows as a swelling of eyes, ears and vent, and in the course of a few days the eyes fill with pus and the rabbit loses its sight. Although affected rabbits continue to feed, they become thin and death usually follows. It is generally understood that the disease is spread by fleas and mosquitoes and since rabbits are gregarious by nature their close contact with each other automatically ensures the rapid spread of the disease. During their suffering the rabbits often become flyblown and this adds to their distressing appearance.

In the first outbreak it was estimated that no more than one per cent of the entire rabbit population survived, and these few were either immune or out of contact with other rabbits. In 1954 the rabbit population had started to rebuild and the Pest Act of that year required all landowners to eliminate wild rabbits. With rabbit numbers low, this was seen as the opportunity for a further reduction but in response to public outcry legislation was also introduced making it illegal to spread myxomatosis by artificial means – by taking infected rabbits and releasing them near disease-free colonies.

Rabbit clearance societies were formed, there was liaison between the Ministry of Agriculture, Fisheries and Food, landowners and farmers and a grant of 50 per cent of all campaign costs was provided. At the same time a Ministry subsidy was introduced on the cost of cartridges used for rabbit and pigeon clearance.

Later, when Ministry support was withdrawn, pest control officers were appointed by the farming community, their work being costed on a price-per-acre basis. There was no obligation for all landowners to take part and the effort came to nothing because it was too thinly spread to be effective. Rabbits, instead of being continually reduced, began to increase in numbers.

Even through the years before myxomatosis rabbits were vulnerable to disease simply because there were so very many of them. They were especially prone to liver problems, mostly seen as enlargements and sometimes as whitish spots. These were seldom fatal, affecting mainly rabbits some eight weeks old, and in the main they recovered. Liver fluke is another disorder which affects them. Many rabbits become heavily infested with tapeworms, which can grow to a length of several feet, but this, surprisingly, doesn't seem to affect their general condition.

The public outcry at the sight of myxomatosis-infected rabbits wandering helplessly around continued since they often strayed into areas where the full extent of their suffering was visible. Their general emaciation and pitiful appearance was such that many people's appetite for rabbits died then and has never returned. Although the demand for rabbit meat has shown some improvement, the general attitude of the consumer has helped to keep demand at a much lower level than previously. As a result rabbiting itself became less popular.

Ten years ago – periodic outbreaks apart – the worst was over. Stocks are now generally big enough to sustain rabbiting in all its forms. In some areas numbers have, in fact, returned to pest proportions – which has to be good news for the sportsman.

The effect of myxomatosis spread far beyond the rabbit. The number of buzzards, whose primary food has always been rabbits, dropped significantly and is only now showing signs of recovery. Foxes became much more wide-ranging in their search for food, since they also depended to a large extent upon rabbits. Not only did the foxes spread more widely across the whole of Britain but they increased their interest in game-bird stocks. In East Norfolk, for example, where I live, I have seen the fox population increase very substantially indeed since that time and this cannot be coincidental.

Rabbits have a supreme facility for survival. They have no specific food requirement and wild rabbits have no significant water intake. They obtain most of the liquid they need through the intake of green vegetation. They can, therefore, exist quite happily in areas of sparse vegetation. Such places as sand dunes along the seashore would seem to be virtual deserts in terms of the food and water on offer, but rabbits will travel considerable distances to feed. There is, in fact, virtually no area at all where rabbits cannot exist – they can support themselves on the edge of suburban Britain and maintain vast colonies on the most inhospitable heathland. Their need for food is easily met and the food we grow for ourselves on agricultural land is little more than a readily-available bonus. If farming ended tomorrow rabbits would increase still further. They would not decline.

They don't readily take to water – but will swim if the necessity arises. They take up residence in some numbers in marsh and swampland. Some of their burrows in low-lying places may at times become very wet but the rabbits usually stay in residence, apparently by no means inconvenienced. They have no dislike of getting their feet wet, while preferring to stay dry where the easy option exists.

They make their home in cliffs, in rocks, in high places – virtually everywhere, in fact – and have the ability to wrest their food from even the most inhospitable of locations. I am sure that in winter rabbits feed twice a night. I have proved this to some extent by night netting, when I have found I could get a double catch off the same ground by netting both before and after midnight in the same night.

Once aware of easy feeding – a field of turnips, for example – a rabbit will travel as much as two or three fields, crossing hedgerows, to take advantage of the situation. In winter rabbits are almost nocturnal in their feeding habits, but come summer and the shortened hours of darkness they are readily seen feeding in the evenings and at daybreak as well as at night. Immature rabbits will, in fact, feed at any time, night and day.

It is those young rabbits, the timid ones afraid to venture too far from home, that are responsible for the massive damage to crops located near woods, hedges and burrows. Adults travel further and feed at random much more freely, and the damage they do is not so noticeable since it is more widespread.

Cereal and root crops are equally vulnerable to rabbit damage. Their favourites are sugar beet, turnips and swedes where these are still available. They have little interest in potatoes but have a great regard for brassicas of all descriptions: cabbages, kale, sprouts, cauliflowers, and the like.

Their damage to cereals is mainly in the spring when the young rabbits are most numerous, but they are not often credited for the plus side of their food intake. They often eat weeds and weed seeds and their economy of intake is illustrated by the fact that they consume their own droppings. They have a lavatorial system – located often on hillocks – where dense concentrations of droppings can be seen. Consumption usually takes place when the droppings are moist. When they are dried out this generally indicates that they have already been eaten twice. Usually these second droppings are much more random and are not often confined to the widely-used lavatorial system.

During the summer months, the times of reproduction, there is ample food available to sustain the increased need, but when winter comes not only does food cease to be so readily available here, there and everywhere but the intake itself has to be much more varied.

Site of rabbits' communal toilet. The droppings will be eaten by the rabbits before they have dried.

During sustained spells of hard weather the rabbit has problems, but it remains thoroughly adaptable to the changed circumstances. It then eats dry instead of green grass if that is a necessity and when snow covers the landscape for many days at a time the rabbit has its own solution.

It then feeds quite heavily on the bark of selected small trees and shrubs. In fact this is a debit side to the food intake. Fruit farmers suffer when apple-tree bark is removed since the loss of a large section around the trunk will kill the tree. This can, of course, be prevented by the provision of rabbit guards of wire netting encircling the whole orchard or individual trees. For small trees there are also a number of plastic guards available. Nothing is perfect. If the complete orchard is enclosed with wire, snow can build up and allow access over the top, especially when drifting occurs. On the other hand, if the mesh is too big, small rabbits can squeeze through, take their fill and become unable to squeeze back, and so are forced to take up residence inside.

The fattest rabbits in winter are often found in close proximity to brambles. At this time brambles are dormant, the sap is within the ground and the brambles themselves have become dry. On eating dry food the rabbit's digestive system slows down, the food is longer within the stomach and greater value is therefore extracted. This automatically ensures the rabbits stay in good condition even with a reduced bulk intake.

Where root crops are fed on the ground to cattle the rabbit has easy pickings and it remains interested and satisfied with the debris littering a field that once held a root crop. The leaves and small fragments of the sugar beet or swede are of obvious value until such time as the field is deep-ploughed and the remaining food buried beyond retrieval. In any case, being such great travellers, rabbits soon locate an alternative source of food.

A healthy rabbit can, if obliged, go a considerable time without food of any sort. On one occasion I recall having a rabbit sealed in a single hole. I knew it was inside, set a trap within the hole and then blocked up the entrance. It was eleven days before that rabbit came to the trap. Rabbits don't store food so it had clearly gone all that time without intake. I had inspected the trap every morning.

Wild rabbits can be kept in captivity and eventually tamed, and it is, in fact, because this has happened through the centuries that we now see so many variations. There are black and white rabbits, there are big-eared and small-eared rabbits. As the result of years of breeding and cross-breeding specialised varieties have been attained specific to both size and colour. As a result, commercially farmed rabbits are available, both for meat and hair; the angora is an example. Other breeds have been imported. Of course this taming process has taken many many years. A litter of truly wild rabbits taken into captivity and contained in a hutch cannot be expected to live very long.

2

The Sporting Methods

Rabbits are a pest or a fine sporting possibility depending on your point of view. They breed and multiply at speed and to cope with their ability to sustain their population a number of rabbit-killing methods have evolved by which the stock can be drastically reduced. These methods, it must be said, result in this big rabbit-population reduction only if they are carried out efficiently. In many instances this has never been the case, which has left the door open for people who regard rabbits as a pest to use the most drastic and least sporting methods.

I know that sporting methods of control can be effective. I have conclusively proved that in my lifetime, and for that reason I can totally oppose the use of gas – gassing rabbits down their burrows – as a means of control. It is wasteful of the meat and wasteful of the sport; it is contemptuous of the rabbit, which is dismissed as a plague, as totally unwanted.

It therefore becomes our responsibility to do our work well at all times to ensure that we achieve what we set out to do if we want to end gassing and to increase the sporting prospects. We must, in fact, achieve what we set out to do or we are of no value to those who permit us on their land. There is a clear message here for all potential rabbiters and sportsmen. Learn your trade fully, do the job properly – no half measures. Take the sport seriously or don't bother with it at all.

It was, in fact, the professional warrener, the man who became each estate's killing machine, who perfected the various sporting methods that exist today and who honed them to their maximum effectiveness. One of the older professional methods, the use of the gin trap, has been phased out and is no longer allowed by law. That leaves a number of perfectly acceptable alternatives which the professional uses in season to the best advantage. There are times and situations where one method becomes favourite compared with the others because of seasonal circumstances and variations in the terrain.

The gin trap has been replaced by other traps which may not be as effective but which are more humane. They kill a very high percentage of their catch immediately, fewer rabbits escape from them and, while killing the rabbit, they do less damage to it. It remains in good condition from the marketing point of view.

Trapping and snaring are both professional methods of rabbit control. Both are very effective but can hardly be rated sporting in our terms. They are effective, yes, but like gassing they can almost be eliminated if we use our sporting methods with greater skill.

The sportsman chooses between rough shooting; a combination of ferreting and shooting or netting; the day and night netting of rough rabbits; and the use of running dogs, such as lurchers for example, both in daylight and after dark, the latter, since lights are used, being known as lamping. I include netting as a sport since in my view, it is undoubtedly that but it is also a very professional method of getting to grips with the stock.

There is the option between day and night netting, when rabbits are flushed forward and are driven into standing nets in which they become entangled. Net systems can extend from as little as 50 yards (45.7 metres) to as long as is manageable. Multiple nets may be extended to become hundreds of yards long for a single operation. In addition, nets can be used in box fashion both in conjunction with ferreting and when rough shooting to completely clear one patch at a time in areas of dense cover.

Box netting completely confines a given area; the rabbits inside have no escape. It therefore offers an opportunity to kill all rabbits confined within that area by the full variety of methods available. Done really effectively there should be few, if indeed any, survivors and by a continuation of this method big areas of woodland can be tackled efficiently.

A percentage of all rabbits stay above ground during daylight. They find themselves cover in secluded areas, adopting a temporary home which they may use on a number of occasions. This is known as a 'seat' and, being partially hidden, it gives them a sense of security. They sit tight, are unlikely to budge unless really disturbed and can be easily shot with a ·22 rifle or even a high-powered air rifle.

Typical long-netting scene, dissecting woodland for daylight netting.

A rabbit on its 'seat', the resting place often used during daylight and the alternative to remaining below ground.

The seat itself. Its shape and worn appearance confirm that it is used regularly.

The advantage of daylight shooting with a rifle comes at dusk and dawn, when substantial numbers of rabbits may be out feeding. Then it is possible to be selective by shooting the adults only. The immature rabbits are ignored.

The use of a shotgun for rabbit clearance, as opposed to the fun of the occasional shot, continues to be less effective than the rifle and especially so when it is used by individuals rather than in conjunction with an organised rough rabbit shoot.

Fully-organised rabbit shoots involve a number of people. A beating system is employed so that some rabbits, especially those that escape behind the beaters, are shot while others are flushed forward to be killed by carefully-positioned waiting guns. The rabbits are, of course, moving targets and in such circumstances the shotgun is effective whereas the rifle would fail.

Rough rabbit shooting conflicts with game shooting in most areas and for that reason is relegated to the months of February and March each year. Night shooting, usually with a ·22 rifle or shotgun, comes into its own after harvest and continues until such time as the winter-sown corn has grown too tall for the rabbits to be seen.

A silenced ·22 rifle is the best weapon, especially when low-powered ammunition is used with it. Not only is it quiet but it doesn't frighten the rabbits in the way a shotgun does. With a rifle a rabbit is either killed or missed. If missed, it is rarely frightened since the silencer ensures that there is no report, so a second, successful, shot is often possible. This means that it is possible to kill many more rabbits in one field at any one time with a rifle than can ever be accomplished with a shotgun. The shotgun may kill the first but it will scare away most if not all of the others.

The ·22 has other advantages. There is increased range flexibility, it is cheaper shot for shot and it leaves a much more saleable end-product.

Running dogs offer an especially sporting approach, I think, but dogs working in this way are not really an effective method of combating heavy infestations of rabbits. And, of course, there is a degree of ground interference which is not conducive to the best interests of the game stock.

Lamping, involving the use of running dogs, is after-harvest night activity which can be continued through the winter in those situations where cover is sparse and where it doesn't interfere with anything else.

Most sporting methods do no more than cream off a proportion of the rabbit stock, but ferreting, to my mind, is the ultimate. This method, if carried out properly, really does reduce the stock. No

Bright-eyed and ready to go again. Note the correct hold.

method is likely to eradicate the stock altogether, for which we should be grateful. But, while it is an extremely sporting and enjoyable method, ferreting involves a lot of hard graft and a lot of skill and knowhow is required if it is to be done effectively.

Rabbits can either be bolted with loose ferrets or be dug out with the assistance of line ferrets, the line being used to indicate the precise location of the quarry.

In simple terms it might well be better for rabbits to be killed while they are very young to eliminate the increased problem that follows from their reproduction. But, of course, rabbits are a commercial as well as a sporting crop and on that basis most efforts at containing their numbers are carried out when the bulk of the rabbits are likely to be mature. Campaigns against them must, however, also be waged at such time as the conditions on the land are suitable. So the generally-applied killing time, regardless of the method to be used by sportsmen, is in the period from August to April – when the rabbits are more mature as a stock and also at their most numerous.

3

Tools of the Trade

A number of very specialist tools are required in the sport of rabbiting, and ferreting in particular. These have been especially designed for the work and it helps to make every effort to obtain them. They are all labour-saving and functionally efficient.

Locating Devices

These include the specialist locating devices that enable the ferret's progress underground to be monitored and its exact position to be discovered. There is the transmitter either worn within the ferret's collar or attached to it and there is the receiving device which the

There are a number of locator devices available, with little to choose between the best.

handler uses. This picks up the transmitter's signal and makes it audible to our ears when the ferret is within range. To my knowledge there are currently four different makes of locator available. All have the same capability, effectively working in a 6-7-foot (2-metre) range, beyond which no signals can be picked up. All are powered by a single PP9 alkaline battery fitted into the receiver, which should be expected to last a full season of regular work. All are compact devices which fit easily in the pocket; they are comparatively robust but, since they are radio-type equipment, they must be handled fairly carefully. The biggest measures some $5 \times 4 \times 2$ inches ($12 \cdot 5 \times 10 \times 5$ centimetres). Weight is inconsequential.

Each proprietary brand of locator has its accompanying transmitter and it must be said that in all four instances these work better if you use the manufacturer's pairing rather than permutating among the ones available. In my view the transmitter is far better positioned on the ferret's collar, though I acknowledge that some other people prefer for their own reasons to trail the transmitter on the line some twelve inches behind the ferret. They claim that this eliminates the

The locator device gets a new battery . . . just in case.

risk of digging on to the ferret but, in my experience, it may more than occasionally require that you dig another hole. Better to be exactly right first time. The other disadvantage has to be that your ferret must then be a line ferret, and it then suffers the disadvantage of having to pull an obstruction, albeit a small one, around any snag that exists within the burrow. In other words, there is a greater risk of snagging.

To generalise, all four of the transmitters are roughly thimble-sized. All four I am referring to have replaceable batteries – an improvement on earlier models. These are small batteries of the type more normally used in hearing aids. They are 1·5 volts and have a battery life which lasts through three to four months of ferreting. It must be remembered that once these batteries are inserted into the transmitter they begin to function. The only way to switch them off is to remove them. It must also be remembered that the working life of what we might regard as identical batteries tends to vary. Some, no matter what the makers say, are better than others. Therefore, when a battery shows signs of diminishing power and range effectiveness it

A ferret collar with transmitter attached.

makes sense to replace it. The cost is minimal anyway and it is practical to have all equipment functioning to perfection. It is a simple matter to test the battery of the transmitter even before leaving home by carrying out a range check in conjunction with the receiver.

You may think, quite rightly, that you need a spare transmitter but do realise that you cannot store this in your pocket during the ferreting or that will be the transmitter picked up by the receiver! Better to store it well out of range – unless, of course, the battery is left out.

After inserting the battery ensure that the mechanism is waterproof. Wrap insulating tape round the transmitter, covering the entire device to prevent water penetration.

The working position of the transmitter is important. The best position is under the ferret's throat – there it will stay in place and is unlikely to slip. The advantage of this is that since the signal position remains the same the signal too is unchanged. Bear in mind that if you do use the transmitter with a line ferret the line needs to be fastened to the collar to assess the actual working position of the transmitter. The D-ring within the collar automatically pulls into position on one or other of the ferret's shoulders. The deviation of that inch or so is of no consequence.

There is so little to choose between these four locator systems that I have no fixed preference and would not recommend you to buy one rather than any other. All function satisfactorily and everyone's final choice will be a matter of individual preference.

The only potential drawback, and this relates to all four systems, is the presence of iron ore deposits, wire netting or overhead high-voltage cables close to or within the working area. All of these can interfere with the signal so that it can be misread. Alas, there is no way this can be overcome but it occurs so rarely that it is not in itself an outstanding problem. The simple solution is to revert to the multiple-dig method, since the next burrow may well not present the same problem. Wire netting in effect works as an aerial, transmitting false radio signals as well as those from the transmitter – with music the most common form of interference.

It wasn't until the early 1950s that ferreters began to receive the benefits of locator systems. Up to that point it was multiple-dig and manual listening only. The first system was an adaptation of the GPO fault-tracing device for underground cables. This consisted of one box with a battery connected to the thin electric cable that was also the ferret's line. Another almost identical box, with attached headphones, was moved over the ground and a continual tone was emitted. When the tone stopped you had reached the end of the line – and that indicated the ferret's position.

These devices never really caught on. There were weaknesses – batteries were neither so good nor so light as they are today and in any case this was the first step. Improvements followed. There seems little doubt that all over the country inventive minds were working on the problem in different ways but the solution came in an unusual fashion. A Scottish firm had produced a transmitter enclosed within a golf ball to enable golfers to locate their wayward shots. Balls often fell into dense cover and if too much time was wasted in retrieval other golfers were delayed. So the transmitter made its debut in sporting terms – and failed to make much impact with the golfing fraternity. Because of the short life of the sealed unit built into each ball, it only lasted six months. Thereafter each quite expensive ball-cum-transmitter was no better than a simple ball.

Fortunately, in the early 1970s, this golfing innovation was shown on television in *Tomorrow's World* and was seen by John Lawrence, a local gamekeeper. He saw the possibilities, contacted the manufacturers with the help of the BBC, and as a result was given two sets of the equipment. The transmitters were at that time a completely sealed unit resembling a marble both in size and appearance. They were used for a full ferreting season and instantly replaced the multiple-dig system. In the time that has elapsed since, the receiving units are virtually unchanged, the only modification being the addition of a depth gauge on some models. This was a simple volume control.

The transmitters, however, have changed considerably. A major improvement was the use of a rechargeable battery inside the transmitter, which was recharged via two protruding wires. The biggest advance was the change from a permanent to a replaceable battery, which resulted in the ferret collar-transmitter as we now know it. In my view the one disadvantage still to be overcome is that the receiver is not as waterproof as it really needs to be. In the meantime it makes sense for the unit to be stored in a plastic bag but I do look forward to the perfectly waterproof receiver being available in due course.

Digging Tools

Digging tools must be chosen with great care to make the work as easy as possible. For me there is nothing to beat the renowned Norfolk long spade for much of this work. So far as I am aware it is no longer in production but there must be many thousands in existence and it is a reasonable assumption that many of these are not now being used. They are probably stacked in garden sheds or outhouses gathering rust. It remains only for you to locate one and buy it at a reasonable price. To get one, the best course is to ask at a gunshop, or to advertise. You could be lucky and pick up a good one very cheaply at a sale of farming equipment.

The implement you need has an overall length of some 6 foot 6 inches (2 metres), is ash-handled and has a long, narrow spoon-shaped blade set at a slight angle to the shaft. Being angled, it allows the user to extract soil from a deep hole without the soil sliding off the blade. The cutting edge is also rounded and is reasonably but not dangerously sharp. You may want to use it to chop through modest-sized tree and bush roots so an effective, labour-saving cutting edge is a must. A metal hook at the top end of the handle is used for recovering line from a hole and is also useful for drawing rabbits out of a hole at a distance beyond the length of a man's arm. This is essentially a digging tool but it has another function I have always found particularly useful. I use it as a listening device – a rabbit and ferret locator. The blade is pushed some 10 or 12 inches (30 centimetres) into the ground immediately above the estimated location of the burrow. Then, by putting my ear to the handle, I hear sounds that tell me whether or not the blade is close to either rabbit or ferret.

The blade is repeatedly thrust into the ground in different spots nearby until I get the best possible signal – and when I get that I then know the rabbit and/or ferret is immediately beneath the spade. The ash shaft transmits vibrations and noise and I can actually hear what is happening down below. This is an ability I have developed over many years, starting, of course, at a time when none of the modern locating devices were available. I still like my own method. It nearly always functions. It never breaks down, doesn't need a battery, and there is no additional expense once you own it.

*The three spades needed when ferreting: the Norfolk long spade,
the graft, and the filling-in spade.*

I do realise, though, that I can hardly advise people to do as I did. They probably have neither the time nor the inclination to go through the necessary learning process, and particularly so now that the more modern battery-powered devices are available and are so efficient. I would, therefore, expect every beginner to ferreting to obtain one of these battery-powered locator systems since they really are quite simple to use – and for a beginner especially they save an enormous amount of time.

I also require a short-handled digging spade that is known locally in Norfolk as a graft. This is quicker and easier to use when you first begin to dig the hole down towards your ferret and, hopefully, the rabbits. Like the long spade, the graft has a rounded blade but this is longer than that of the long spade and the taper is sharper. The handle is exactly the same as that of your ordinary garden spade or fork. The hole you dig should be round, not square, since there is much less effort expended in digging a round hole – and if the digging is down through a grassed surface the size of the hole can be anticipated and one complete turf taken out to be replaced later. This makes the ground look as though it had never been disturbed. The graft, like the long spade, has a slightly rounded cutting edge, which again needs to have a good but not a sharp edge to it. Use the graft for the first two or three feet (60 to 90 centimetres) of the hole and thereafter use the long spade.

If I am ferreting single-handedly there is no need for any other digging implement. I have always found that I can fill in easily enough with the graft – and no one wants to be weighed down by the sheer weight of gear to be carried around. Even so, if there are two of you working together an ordinary garden spade or even a shovel can be used by one man to fill in some holes while the other man uses the graft or long spade on a new excavation. It is also more than useful to have a reap-hook with you. It needs to be sharp, of course, since you will use that to clear away surface vegetation and for cutting a route into a hedgerow to obtain easy access to the mouth of a burrow.

Muzzles, Collars and Lines

A muzzle is used to prevent your ferret killing a rabbit as it progresses through the various holes within the warren system bolting as many rabbits as it can. There are a variety of muzzles available. They can be shop-bought in leather, in ring form, or can be home-made. I prefer to make my own, using thin cotton string. This is not too strong and if the ferret should by any chance be lost for any length of time the muzzle rots through and, instead of starving, the ferret is able to hunt and kill for itself. Nylon, of course, never rots and for that reason should not be used as a muzzle material.

I tie my string muzzles to those ferrets that are to be worked loose down the burrows and whose main function is to bolt the rabbits from underground. You need two lengths of soft, cotton-based string between 15 and 18 inches (40 – 45 centimetres).

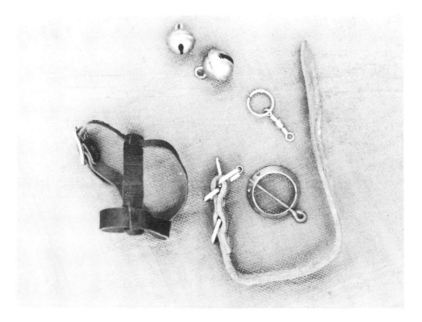

Leather muzzle, brass muzzle, ferret's collar, line swivel and bells. An assortment of accessories, with both muzzles now out of favour.

Remember, nylon will not do. The two lengths of string are held together side by side and are knotted together with two simple bights about an inch apart. This distance is important since it relates to the size of the ferret's head; it can be adjusted slightly if necessary to fit the head of the particular ferret to be used.

Pass the string round the ferret's neck, making sure that one of the knots already tied is located centrally under the neck. The two ends from this knot are then tied on top of the neck. The remaining two ends are now taken around each side of the mouth and are knotted on top of the ferret's head between eyes and nose. Properly done, this prevents the ferret from opening its mouth, but care must be taken to make sure that the animal's whiskers are neither disturbed nor disarranged.

The final move is to tie all four loose ends together at the top of the head. This prevents the muzzle from slipping over the ferret's nose. Cut off the remaining loose ends. This is a two-man

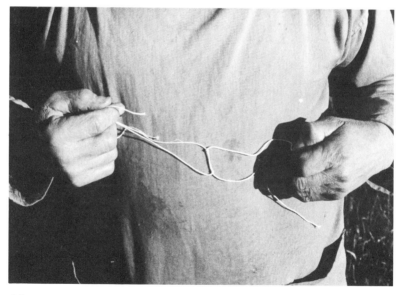

(*a*)

The five stages for making and tying a cotton string muzzle to a loose ferret. Once the tying is mastered, this is the best muzzle available.

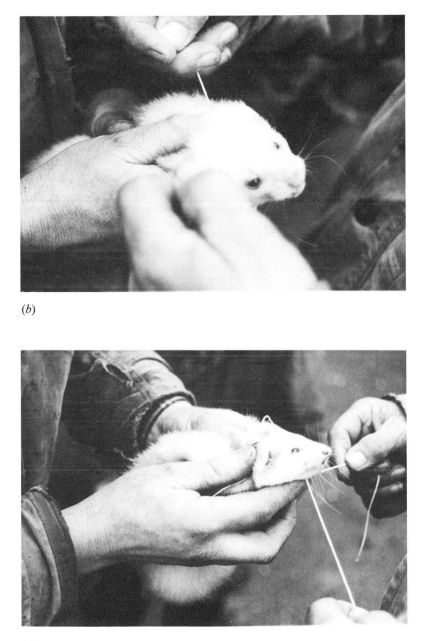

(*b*)

(*c*)

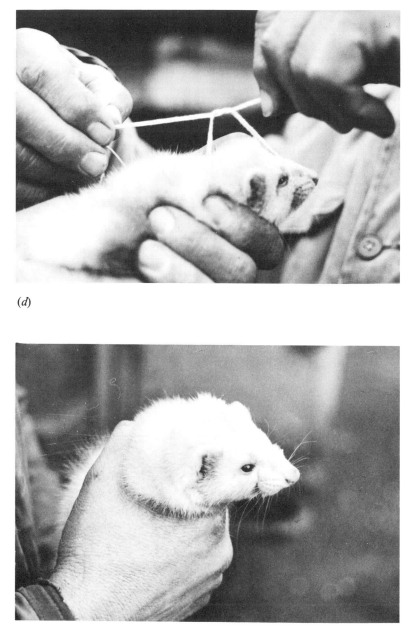

(d)

(e)

job of work since you need one to hold the ferret securely while the other ties the knots. It is all very simple to do but it is crucial that the ferret should not become frightened. It must remain at ease all the time or the task will become more difficult.

That explains why I always establish a friendly relationship with my ferrets. I talk to them while the muzzle is tied in place and they then remain very docile. There's really no chance of getting bitten if your ferrets have been properly handled over a long period and are never scared.

When the time comes to remove the muzzle it is a simple matter to cut the neck strand of the string with a knife and the whole thing then falls free. If the muzzle has been properly tied the ferret will be free to lick but not to bite. This allows it to gather moisture should it become lost; its mouth remains wet and the string is wet too. The softening, rotting process gets under way from the moment the muzzle is first tied in place. The ferret can drink and will live a long time should it escape.

Ferrets must become used to wearing a muzzle long before they are fitted with one for a day's ferreting. I therefore put muzzles on all the ferrets I intend to work loose. They wear these muzzles from time to time so that they become accustomed to the restrictions imposed upon them. I always talk to the ferrets while the muzzles are put in place and try to ensure that they are never frightened. Then when the time comes for them to be worked with muzzles in place and they are released into rabbit burrows they are calm and unworried. They get on with the work required of them instead of concentrating on attempting to remove the muzzle.

There are other less effective muzzles available. There is the metal-ring type muzzle, which is screwed into place via a pin passed across the inside of a ferret's mouth behind its big teeth and then threaded back into the ring. This is effective, I won't deny that. Too effective, for there is no way that muzzle can be removed other than by the handler. If lost, the ferret cannot survive for any length of time. It cannot eat or drink. I believe these muzzles are now illegal.

Then there is the leather-strap type of muzzle. This has the big advantage that it can be put into place by just one person. But even this doesn't overcome my prejudice against the fact that the leather is virtually rotproof. Until it is removed the ferret cannot eat. Other than the three I have described, I know of no muzzles that have any claim to efficiency. I strongly recommend the string type. Learn to tie it and you will realise there is nothing better.

Good-quality collars can be bought at virtually every gunshop but do ensure that a top-quality swivel is located between the collar D and the line itself. This prevents the line from kinking. The best line is of braided nylon, which doesn't absorb water and become heavy. It is rotproof and reliable. The line should be some 10 or 12 yards (9 or 10 metres) long and it should be marked off from the collar in distances of 1, 2 and 5 yards (0.9, 1·8 and 4·5 metres). The line itself must be securely tied or spliced to the swivel. As additional security I always sew mine, with the ends of the nylon melted with a lighted match to prevent fraying. It is important that the ferrets should not become upset or bewildered and, just as I condition my loose ferrets to muzzles before working them while wearing one, I find that it pays to give line ferrets the opportunity to become accustomed to both collar and line. They will work so much better on the day if they are given that advance preparation.

Nets

Another essential aspect of rabbit clearance when this is to be done without the use of guns is nets. Two types are used: purse nets and long-nets. Purse nets are used to cover all holes leading to and from a warren system. In every major burrow there is a main entrance-cum-exit and in addition there may be more entrances and a number of emergency exits.

It is preferable for every hole to be covered with a purse net if a gun is not being used. This may be difficult when the warren is very large and a corresponding number of purse nets is needed but when working on burrow systems, rather than on the much larger warrens, twenty nets are often sufficient. The ferrets are slipped under the nets and the nets then replaced behind them. When the rabbits are bolted they emerge from the exit holes – and entrances too – at some speed. The impact tightens the purse net as the draw cord pulls tight and the rabbit is trapped. Before the rabbit is taken out of the net, another net should be set over

A purse net positioned and staked over an inconspicuous bolt-hole.

The purse net functions perfectly and the rabbit is enveloped and helpless.

the hole in case other rabbits bolt.

I prefer my purse nets to have a knot-to-knot measurement of $2\frac{1}{8}$ inches (5·4 centimetres). This allows a smallish ferret to pass through the mesh. I make my own purse nets but some of good quality can be bought from all well-stocked gunshops. Buy the number you can afford, but I believe that anyone working seriously needs to have some thirty purse nets with him during each day's work. There are times when many more will be very useful.

Shop-bought purse nets can have their limitations. I have sometimes found that they are longer than need be but not wide enough. As the result they do not sit very effectively over a bolt-hole. I make my own – at a fifth of the cost of the shop-bought article. My own purse nets are much rounder in shape and I am sure that is what's needed since, after all, the rabbit hole is generally round.

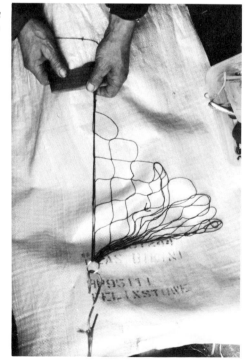

Bob Smithson makes his own purse nets. Here's one under construction.

Long-nets have a number of uses. They can be used to completely encompass a big warren system, they can be used to divide up areas of woodland and they can be operated both at night and by day when conditions are favourable. But although long-nets have a number of uses the nets are exactly the same for each purpose. When a ring of netting is placed round a warren, all bolting rabbits must be caught provided that they are not able to get back into the burrow. Every one that hits the net ought to be caught – provided the net has been set properly.

A long-net, when pegged out, should stand 2 foot 6 inches (0·75 metres) off the ground. It can be 100 yards long, even more if two or more nets are joined together. But 100 yards is the standard length of a long-net and as a general rule this length suffices. A good-quality 100-yard long-net today will have a long working life and is fairly expensive, but 50-yard and even 20-yard nets are useful at times, especially when working hedgerows. As with purse nets, I prefer to make my own, each long-net having a 2-inch (5-centimetre) knot-to-knot diameter.

A long-net is erected in front of a wood to demonstrate its appearance.

Modern nets are available both in nylon and in hemp – although hemp is going out of fashion. That's a pity for there is no doubt at all that hemp nets hang better and catch better. The only advantage of nylon is that it is longer-lasting. It is rotproof but then if hemp nets are properly dried after every occasion when they get damp or wet there will be no problem. One disadvantage of nylon is that the knots are inclined to slip, creating variations in mesh size.

Stakes are needed to support the long-net. You can reckon to need twenty to support a 100-yard net, allowing a few spares to be on the safe side and to allow for breakage. I use hazel stakes, cut in the autumn after the sap has receded. They are then green and easy to cut and shape into good straight sticks. They need to be 3 feet (1 metre) long and with a sharp point fashioned at one end. A blunt point is difficult to push into hard ground. After I have cut, straightened and sharpened the stakes I put them away to dry out and stiffen – to season – before they are used. Good stakes can last a long time, but it does help if they are cut some months before they are used, and well seasoned.

Use long-pointed, seasoned stakes. These penetrate the ground with minimal effort.

Shotguns

There is an argument to support virtually every gauge of shotgun that can be used to kill rabbits bolted from burrows. I don't suggest that this is a very crucial question and everyone is really free to use the gun he prefers since they will all do the job. If the ferreting is in a confined space then a 4·10 is a useful weapon. I have shot thousands of rabbits with a 4·10, often from a perch in the fork of a tree with a dog hunting thick cover below. At close range head shots can be made which will not inflict too much damage to the rabbits.

The more powerful 12-bores are, of course, needed for open warren shooting, but a 1oz (25g) load cartridge is always likely to be heavy enough. Other bores can also be used but the obvious point must be that a small charge in the right place is a lot better than a heavier charge badly directed.

The ideal shot size has to be no. 6 and 7 for a 12-bore, with the no. 6 getting my vote for use with a 4·10. Bear in mind that this is often quite close-range shooting, often little if any more than 20 yards (18 metres). A 4·10 is of doubtful advantage at more than 25 yards (22·5 metres) but up to that point can be a very good gun in the right hands. Open-bored guns are best; true cylinder and improved are ideal, I think. Nothing over ¼ choke is needed.

4
Ferrets –
Their Care and Training

The ferret is a member of the weasel family, and the weasel, stoat, polecat and ferret are all animals with a natural hunting instinct and are not deterred by working underground. The ferret's function is to frighten the rabbits so that they bolt out of the holes or to force them to retreat through the burrow system until they become cornered so that they can be dug out while the ferret holds them in that fixed position.

The origins of the ferret as a hunting animal are obscure. Man could have had little if any need for ferrets until the arrival of rabbits here in Britain. It is not, though, beyond the bounds of possibility they were used to control the large numbers of rats that inhabited the countryside in the Middle Ages and thereafter. It may be that ferrets, like rabbits, were imported into this country from Europe. However, it is my belief that when rabbits were introduced here and multiplied they were then predated upon by animals already resident. Stoats, weasels and polecats were the more obvious of these and man, being the innovator that he is, may well have captured, tamed and adapted some of these animals for his own purposes over a period of centuries. They could have been caught while young and retained in captivity, and as the result of hand-feeding and regular handling they would eventually have become quite domesticated.

Breeding in captivity followed and the progeny progressively became more and more reconciled to the life that ferrets have today. The exact origins of the ferret can only be guesswork, but either descendants of the polecat line or variations on the resultant interbreeding between stoats and polecats may have given us the ferret we know today. It is a well-known fact that ferrets have mated with polecats in the wild. Variations in size, shape and colour are merely peculiarities of the original, as can

46

be seen in many other wild and domesticated species. As a small boy I recall a very old gamekeeper (at least, he seemed old to me at the time) talking of gypsies having tame stoats in captivity.

Acquiring Ferrets

So, first obtain your ferrets. As with all living creatures, there are good and bad, suitable and unsuitable, and it figures that you must invest in animals capable of doing the work required of them. In that respect the best advice I can offer is to ensure that they come from good working stock. In other words, they need to have been parented by ferrets which themselves have been used extensively for ferreting so that the inborn instincts remain strong. So the best source from which to obtain your ferrets has to be someone deeply committed to the animals, someone who keeps his own working and breeding stock and who from time to time may have a surplus. A warrener is, of course, the ideal man.

Out of his professional need, he will have settled on a good working strain over the years and any surplus he may have is virtually guaranteed to be first-class. You can buy from him in complete confidence. Since his surplus stock may be in keen demand he may not be able to supply you – but he can at least point you in the right direction by suggesting alternative sources, ones that have proved themselves so far as he is concerned.

There was a firm belief among old-time ferreters that the ferrets needed to be vicious and half-starved to do their work well. It was thought that only animals of that description could either eject rabbits from their burrows or kill them underground. There is the folklore assertion that when an experienced warrener went to buy ferrets at a market his first action on inspecting them was to insert his hand in a cage containing a number of the animals. Those that bit him and hung on to his hand were the ones he bought. What incredible logic!

It must surely be much more pleasant and by no means as painful to work with friendly and docile ferrets. I am certain that a half-starved ferret has neither the strength nor the stamina to do a reasonable day's work. And, of course, if the ferret is half-starved its first and understandable reaction on encountering a rabbit in a burrow is to kill immediately and then to settle down and eat it. The result at the very least is wasted time – and the rabbit is damaged to the point where it is unlikely to be saleable.

Anyone setting out to equip himself fully needs the barest minimum of two ferrets. Four is a much more logical number and if the hobby is to be taken very seriously, with regular work for the ferrets available, there could well be a need for six. It is obvious from the outset that some ferrets are more capable workers than others. Perseverance must prevail so that all your ferrets become proficient. It is sometimes convenient to overwork the most efficient to the point where they become exhausted, but this is the quickest way to introduce bad habits such as leaving a kill or disregarding a rabbit tucked up at the end of a hole.

After April, ferrets are often available from individuals at giveaway prices. The ferreting season has just ended and those people with no more than a passing interest, perhaps a failed interest, will then be keen to dispose of their stock rather than feed and maintain them to the start of another season. Bargains are available provided you can be sure that the animals come from good stock and have been kept in good condition.

Ferreting is once again increasing in popularity. There was an inevitable lack of interest when rabbit stocks fell after myxomatosis, and after a very short time there was a corresponding fall in the number of ferrets retained for sporting purposes. Ferret stocks have now been rebuilt sufficiently for them to be fairly readily available for those in need.

There is, in effect, only one ferret – but there are broad variations within the species. These variations do not jeopardise the animals' ability to do their work well, provided the strain is a good one. For example, I have heard one variation described as the greyhound ferret – this is a long, slim variety with a sharp-featured head. In addition, there are large, small, narrow-headed, short and broad-headed animals. None of this matters at all provided the ferrets work efficiently. Some people have their own preference, of course, but I have never thought that one variation works better than any other. It all depends on each individual animal.

Colours are also varied. The majority are either white or the natural colours of the polecat (black and ginger), but there are

A line ferret being prepared for duty.

A loose ferret is off to work.

also cross colourings between the two that have white undercoats and overriding gingery hairs. All colours have their plus and minus points and there are times when a particular colour is best. The white ferret, for example, is more visible, while the polecat is less so.

Different areas around the country give different names to the sexes. For example, a male ferret can be either a hob or a jack, while a female is a bitch or a jill. The males are usually used as line ferrets and the females are worked loose, muzzled or otherwise. A young animal can begin its working life at six months old.

It must be mentioned, too, that there is an ever-increasing tendency for ferrets to be kept purely as pets. Ferret societies have been formed and their numbers are increasing. There is, in fact, a ferret corner with animals on display at most country fairs and they do attract wide interest. I suppose that ferrets are no more unusual as pets than rats, snakes and goodness only knows what else. All depends on what appeals to the individual, but I must say that ferrets always respond to good treatment and, given that, there is never any reason to fear them. My own ferrets are in fact retained for working purposes – but I would have to admit that, yes, they are probably pets too.

Housing

All your ferrets can be housed together – provided that the hutch is big enough. The exception is at breeding time when the female comes into season. At that time it makes good sense to separate males from females.

So far as the ferrets' accommodatioin is concerned, I prefer a roomy hutch with separate sleeping quarters. One to house four ferrets should not be less than 3 feet (1 metre) tall at the front and have a sloping roof. The floor area will be some 4×3 feet (1·25× 1 metre) and the hutch will be sited outside, not inside any other building. The most important single aspect of siting is that the

Typical ferret hutch with low-level doors for easy access and cleaning.

hutch must be positioned so that it does not receive direct sunlight. Sunshine and any form of overheating affects fur growth, especially in the young animals. If overheating occurs ferrets are far less likely to grow their winter coat so readily.

The sleeping quarters should measure 18 inches (45 centimetres) by the full width of the floor space. The run section is faced with small-meshed wire netting or with Twillweld, and the facing side is 3 feet (1 metre) tall to ensure that a big area of wire mesh is available. The ferrets will like to climb on this and while doing so will clean their feet. Hinged doors opening outwards from floor level facilitate easy cleaning and the hutch must be constructed to stand off the floor, preferably on legs, to ensure that urine and surplus drinking water drain away easily so that the floor remains dry. The floor must be lined with straw

A wire-mesh front to the hutch helps keep the place airy and the ferrets' feet clean.

within the sleeping quarters but wood shavings can be used within the run section since this is easier to clean out – a task that must be carried out regularly. Good pine shavings are best as they contain resin, which also acts as an insect repellent. Oak shavings, for instance, soon turn black when wet.

The division between the sleeping and run sections is fitted at floor level with a hole just large enough to allow the ferrets easy passage but small enough to prevent them dragging food carcasses from the run section into the sleeping quarters.

Feeding

It pays not to overfeed adult ferrets at times when they are not working or they become fat and lazy. I prefer flesh-fed ferrets. During my time as a gamekeeper I almost always had a supply of fresh meat available to give them. This included rabbits, pigeons, and even clean rats and winged vermin. Offal, obtained from the butcher's shop, is an easily available substitute for those lacking the supplies available to me. Some prefer other food. Milk-based diets or scalded biscuit meal and dried meat and eggs are good occasional alternatives. Clean drinking water must be available at all times. A hutch containing four mature working ferrets should have not less than 1lb (450g) of fresh meat daily – that's the equivalent of half a rabbit.

Breeding

A one-year-old ferret can be mated. As soon as a female begins to swell up and start coming into season she should be taken away from the males and kept separately. When she is fully in season she is ready to be mated and the chosen male is introduced. Mating takes place almost immediately. The male can be left with the female, probably mating her two or three times, but this is of no importance. After mating she soon goes off heat and the two can remain together if necessary until the fifth week of the gestation period, when the male ferret is removed. Total gestation time is approximately 45 days.

The removal of the male enables the female to settle down in isolation for a week or so prior to giving birth. She will make her nest in the sleeping quarters of the hutch where she will eventually have her litter. The young could number anything from two to well into double figures. Like rabbits, they are born blind but they do have some very fine body hair.

Pregnancy can alter the behaviour of some females. Some previously good-natured, very docile ferrets can become vicious, probably as a defensive measure and as a protection for their young. They must therefore be approached with some apprehension and with rather more care than normal. It is unwise to attempt to handle newly-born ferrets. The mother may object and females have even been known to kill the complete litter in consequence.

When does handling commence? Just as soon as the young ferrets can see and crawl around the nest is the time to make a start. They must be kept scrupulously clean and as soon as they start to feed on flesh – at about three weeks – the nest can be removed and new straw added. At that time the young ferrets are being handled regularly and this process of getting them

Mother's on guard while young ferrets nestle contentedly together.

accustomed to human touch and handling continues through every cleaning-out stage. The result is that the growing ferrets show no shyness to human contact.

The female will leave her own food away from the young where it doesn't contaminate the nest. As their demand for more food arises the young ferrets will then make their way towards the fresh meat, taking a great interest in it. The mother will continue to drag the young ferrets back into the nest but eventually she gives up as their demand for fresh meat increases.

It is essential that flyblown meat is not given as food and it is equally essential to ensure that food given to the young ferrets doesn't subsequently become flyblown. This is because if the hutch becomes infested with maggots there is the possibility that the maggots will penetrate the young ferrets' ears and vent, causing great distress. Therefore, and to counteract this possibility, a good sprinkling of Jeyes Fluid should be applied to the floor of the hutch after cleaning out and before the new straw and shavings are added.

Cleanliness is of great importance at all times. All drinking dishes and all food receptacles must be washed each time before their contents are replenished. Hygiene is the name of the game. Provided the hutch is big enough to allow adequate living space for the female and her young, they can stay together until becoming adult. There are, in fact, times when the young will actually appear to be bigger than their mother. This is due to the fact that the mother will have shed her coat, while the young retain their fluffy coat which appears to increase their body size.

Handling and Familiarisation

Regular handling and fondling of the young animals helps ensure they grow up into docile but nonetheless bold animals. There is nothing worse than a shy ferret. A shy one causes all sorts of complications and can become a great time-waster. One of the problems is that it is much more likely to become hostile and therefore difficult to handle. This can also affect its working life since a shy ferret is reluctant to leave a burrow after its work down there has ended.

So I talk to mine every time I approach the hutch. I call them

Billies regardless of sex, using an amiable tone of voice since it is important they do not become involved in or suffer any hostility of any sort. Mine become so tame that they climb up the inside of the wire mesh when I approach the hutch and are clearly pleased to see me. Everyone who owns ferrets needs to develop this sort of relationship with his animals. It is important because they come to trust you implicitly, and trust is the only sound basis for a good working relationship. Time spent on this aspect is a very sound investment in the ferrets' future performance.

For those who may not know, the correct method of picking up a ferret is to gently place your hand underneath the animal, thumb uppermost, with the front feet of the ferret being between index finger and middle finger. The index finger is thus under the ferret's throat and the thumb goes round the top of the neck. There is no need to exert any pressure. The animal does not need to be restrained in any way. Remember, it is a friend of yours. It will remain docile. It certainly won't bite you. Held in the way described, it cannot move its front legs and that means that it is unable to scratch you even should it want to. In fact, holding a ferret in this way is very convenient for muzzling purposes. The key is to be deliberate in your actions. Never be apprehensive or let that apprehension show. Confidence rubs off and pays dividends.

As a general rule ferrets can be expected to live between five and nine years. They become mature and adult for working purposes at about eight or nine months and will continue to work for the duration of their life. It is, of course, desirable they should never be overworked or overstressed, and you can ensure that this does not happen by having a sufficient number so that it is always possible to rest some while using others.

It is also important that my dogs and my ferrets get to know each other long before they are required to work together in the field. In the normal way a ferret meeting a strange dog would become hostile, would hiss and spit. The last thing it would think of would be working. It would be defensive and unsure of itself. So for that reason the two must be introduced to each other and become acquainted. Then there is no possibility of hostility and the two will work together very amiably in response to instructions. This can save a great deal of time when they are being worked in the field.

Ailments

Ferrets are subject to a variety of ailments. Distemper is by far the worst. It is invariably fatal and can wipe out your entire stock. There is no known preventive measure and it simply seems a matter either of good or bad luck whether your ferrets suffer it or not. Dogs, though, can be vaccinated against distemper – so it pays to keep their vaccine boosters up to date. Fortunately I have never had this problem either with ferrets or dogs but should it ever hit my animals it means more than just the loss of the ferrets. The hutches must be burned. They will be so contaminated with the virus that there is nothing else to be done.

Another ferret disease is mange, which affects the animals' feet and tails. These become hairless and develop septic sores. The condition stems from dirty living conditions within the hutches. I have known it to be successfully treated with black sulphur powder mixed with water but prevention is better than cure. If the hutches are cleaned regularly and fresh straw added there is unlikely to be a problem.

Botulism is another fatal disease which has come to the fore in recent years. A friend of mine lost a whole litter by feeding them a wild goose which he thought had died as a result of a collision with overhead power cables. The vet diagnosed botulism so undoubedly the goose was infected.

Rabbit fleas must get on to ferrets from time to time. These do not usually cause a problem as they leave ferrets as quickly as they leave humans. If fleas or mites persist they can be easily dealt with by a fly spray. Ticks are often found on ferrets. Don't pull them off but dab them with a little paraffin.

Unmated Females

In recent years there has been an ongoing controversy relating to unmated females. It has been suggested that unless females are mated they remain in season for very long periods and lose condition and strength to the point where they die. That is not my experience. Occasionally one will die. Occasionally members of all species die when out of condition for no known reason. Whether such a ferret fatality can be attributed to it remaining unmated is highly debatable. I have proved this theory wrong to my own satisfaction having kept females together for a matter of years, in which time they were never mated. The fact is that I have not needed a constant stream of young ferrets. One litter a year is quite enough for my needs, and it is in any case very much better to look after one litter properly – it may number eight or a dozen – than to spread the effort (and the food available) through a much larger number.

Ferret Boxes

On the working day you will need a method of transporting your ferrets from their hutch to the area where they will be used. In my view nothing betters a good ferret box. This is a lightweight wooden construction and has a hinged lid, secured with a hasp and a small wooden peg. Attach the peg to the box with a short length of cord – losing it can be irritating.

Ferret boxes can be made in a variety of sizes. They can be partitioned to accommodate ferrets singly or in multiples as necessary. If I am to take four ferrets with me, my preference is for one box with one partition and two ferrets in each compartment. If, on the other hand, I am taking six ferrets then I need two boxes – one for four as already described and another for the remaining two animals.

Essentials include a good-quality, wide carrying-strap and a sufficient number of approximately ½-inch (1·25-centimetre) breather holes bored at each end. The boxes are lined with either straw or wood shavings, not only so that the ferrets can be transported in comfort over bumpy farm tracks and fields, but also so that they can relax in comfort during the periods of rests after working. There need be no provision for either food or water during the average working day. I like to keep my ferrets sharp and that means marginally under feeding them the day before they are to be used. On their return home after a day's work they must then be given a good if not excessive meal.

Some people carry their ferrets around in bags or sacks. Not for me. I prefer my ferrets to have the benefit of a flat base where they can lie down in comfort. Sacks are not waterproof and offer only limited protection from a cold wind. A box, on the other

An assortment of well-ventilated ferret carrying-boxes. Take your pick.

A compartmented ferret box – the ferrets sitting placidly.

hand, offers all-round protection. It is likely to be waterproof and windproof and there is additional protection should someone be foolish enough to fire a shot in the direction of the ferrets' container while bolting rabbits.

5

Where and How to Ferret

So you are now ready to go rabbiting. You have your ferrets, know how to handle them, have all the tools of the trade available and you are raring to go. But to where? First locate the area where you can go rabbiting.

Wherever you go you need permission in writing from whoever has the right to grant it. This may be either the landowner or his tenant, depending on the tenant's occupancy agreement. It may be that all the sporting rights are held by the landowner, that the landowner is the occupier, or that the tenant has all the rights. You must ensure when seeking permission to go rabbiting anywhere that you get the consent from someone legally able to give it to you. And you must be aware of the full extent or limitations of whatever is offered to you.

So you must first ensure that your approach is to the right quarter and you must realise at the outset that mutual trust is essential. This is a situation where you cannot knock on a door and hope to be immediately granted the favours you seek. This has to be a make-haste-slowly situation. You need to know either the landlord or the tenant and, more important, he needs to know you before he can be expected to grant you the right to work on his land. He must know that you can be trusted, otherwise his first and last inclination must inevitably be to turn you down.

Whoever farms the land in question may very well want the rabbits disposed of – but not at the price of constant disturbance of his land and perhaps at the risk of the well-being of the game shooting. This is such a complex matter, with so many variations to take into account, that it is in your own interest to act slowly. Take your time, build up a case, establish the right relationships and you are halfway there.

Various arrangements can be made. Sometimes the farmer will be almost desperate to be rid of his rabbits since he regards them as a pest which makes undesirable inroads into the profitability of his farm. In such cases you may have to do little more than convince the farmer you can do the job – and do it well. He may let you do everything you ask: use a gun, use dogs, use nets, come and go as you please – and retain all the rabbits you kill totally without cost. This may be the more usual situation but few people would give such freedom to total strangers.

Ground can sometimes be hired on a commercial basis but it is more often totally free of charge provided the farmer is assured of your good character and dependability. Game shooting is very often the primary sporting consideration and this can mean that those who want the rabbiting rights may have to accept restrictions on time and place – on guns and dogs too. There are other, much rarer situations where the farmer is totally uninterested in any sporting aspects. His abiding concern is his farm and if you can convince him that you can efficiently dispose of the rabbits on his property he may be more than pleased to welcome you.

My own ferreting campaigns begin in October but from that time onward to the end of the game-shooting season I am limited to outside hedgerows and warrens and burrows well away from the standing crops of game cover and the woods. Only after 1 February can I go more or less where I please and then there is a need to work quite quickly since the ferreting season ends in April when the fast-growing vegetation and the increasing arrival of litters of young rabbits make it impractical to continue.

So, you have the rights you sought. What now? First know your boundaries, since you must limit your operations to the exact area allowed to you. Failure to benefit from a complete briefing in that respect can lead to a very rapid termination of your sport, so the onus is on you to ensure that you are fully aware of the exact boundaries. You must talk this subject through very fully indeed with the man concerned, establishing which boundary hedges are his and which belong to his neighbours. A map can be very useful if there is one available, or a conducted tour of the land, but it is your responsibility to ensure that you stay within the limits of the concessions that have been made to you. Start off properly and you have a much better chance of being welcome year after year.

It goes without saying, almost, that you need to be generous with the rabbits you kill. Maybe the farmer or his tenant will ask for a percentage of the kill within the agreement, but it makes jolly good sense to ensure that anyone who likes to eat a rabbit and who can influence your sport is well looked after.

So you now survey the land at your disposal. You simply walk the land, survey the warren and burrow systems and get some knowledge that will help you plan where and how to make your first move against the rabbit population. Where should you start? That's a complex question indeed if you have a lot to learn.

Most amateur ferreters want a quick killing. They want as many rabbits as possible for the minimum amount of effort and time commitment. That's perfectly understandable, but it's not good sense. Sometimes, as a matter of necessity, you must tackle the harder terrain first. In practice it pays to start on the bigger warren systems rather than on the smaller isolated burrows with their limited number of entrances and bolt holes.

If you start with the harder work, those rabbits that are not killed will move into the smaller systems. They will be relatively easy to dispose of once the big warrens have been worked out and closed down. But if you start with the easy places the surviving rabbits move into harder ground and you may never get them out. So, on that basis, it makes good sense to start on the bigger warrens.

It may be useful if I define a warren. This is a major system of burrows, all interlinking so that it becomes necessary to work on all aspects of the warren at one time. The burrow, on the other hand, may be just one section of a warren or it may be a single burrow system which is much smaller than a warren and exists in isolation from other rabbit holes.

Some warrens are so extensive they can range over as much as 50 acres or take in a complete gravel working. These will have a larger, even a massive number of entrances and bolt-holes and it is first of all very important to be able to distinguish between the entrances and exits. The entrances can be defined as those holes exhibiting quantities of scraped-out sand or soil around them, whereas a bolt or exit hole is simply that, a hole in the ground with no other clue to its whereabouts than that hole.

Bear in mind that big warrens are time-consuming. Complex

situations can develop. This means that you should plan to start work on a big system early in the day and keep at it until at least a complete section of the warren has been dealt with. You must tackle a warren as though you intend to do a good job at it; there's precious little point or pleasure in dabbling with it for that way you achieve very little. Remember that if you return home at the end of the session with the work you planned to do uncompleted you cannot expect to return the next day or the next week to find the situation exactly as you left it. The rabbits will have moved out or back – and, in effect, you must start completely from scratch again.

Tidiness is another virtue. It may not catch you many, if any, more rabbits but it looks good. It helps maintain good relations. So always fill in the day's workings before you leave for home, taking special care that there are no holes or pitfalls you have created into which livestock can stray and suffer injury. Be methodical at all times. Be quiet. The less disturbance you make

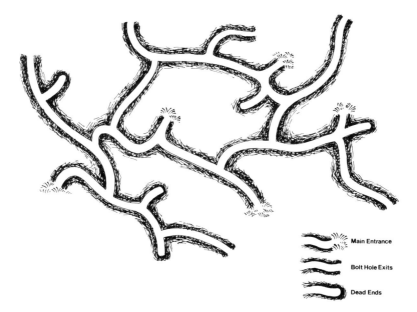

Main Entrance

Bolt Hole Exits

Dead Ends

Typical layout of a rabbit warren, showing the entrances, bolt-holes and dead-ends, all of which figure in the ferreting technique.

the less the rabbits are disturbed – and the pheasants and partridges too.

The more efficient you become the more likely you are to retain the rabbiting rights for the future. Obviously, the farmer sees your success in terms of reduced damage to his crops. Achieve that and do it while respecting all else around you and you are assured of your right to come again.

Experience soon teaches that there are some warren situations which cannot be ferreted. All efforts made will be doomed to failure for a number of reasons. A day's hard work can produce a no-kill result and it is important that everyone should be able to recognise the visible differences between a good and an impossible situation. There are, of course, invisible aspects that make a warren, or at least a section of it, impossible. But let's look first at the visible problems, realising the need for fun, not for a fruitless day's digging or waiting around for ferrets that are none too likely to return to the surface once allowed underground.

The most impossible situation will be fairly obvious – a warren system in a sheer cliff or in a hillside, within a railway cutting or

Four entrances to a relatively small warren. The bolt-holes are inconspicuous.

A large warren with ferreting complicated by trees and bushes.

a quarry. All of these are difficult because it is very unlikely that you will be able to dig down to collect the rabbits that the ferrets accumulate at the dead-ends of the burrows. Many of these warrens will be long-term sites where rabbits may have lived almost unmolested through centuries. It is unlikely you can accomplish what generations of warreners may have looked at and scratched their heads over before moving on. There may well be many entrance holes, many more bolt-holes and every outward sign of rabbit occupation in numbers. This is very possible but, what is clear is that the only course open to you is to introduce your ferrets and hope that they will bolt a reasonable number of the occupants, since the depths involved make digging out impossible.

Where ferreting is curtailed in this way you may be able to trap the entrance holes and snare the nearby runs; you may also be able to crop the rabbits by night netting and by evening and night shooting. But you can never effect a total kill. In some situations of this sort digging out would call for an excavator, not a spade!

The roots of tall standing trees can often present problems when the trees are growing on an embankment. The situation is already difficult because of the steepness of the slope without the complications imposed by the roots. There is no way you can dig around major roots and there, therefore, is another situation in

Root problems can be expected here.

A rabbit warren enlarged by a vixen to serve as a fox earth.

which you are forced to rely on the rabbits being bolted, recognising that you cannot thereafter kill those which remain behind in the system.

However, the complications created by roots are not so acute when the tree is standing on level land. In this situation, if your ferrets are introduced via entrance holes next to the tree's trunk they must, as they progress through the burrow system, move away from the thicker roots. The roots become smaller the further the ferret progresses down the hole away from the tree itself. It is quite likely that when your ferret locates rabbits in a dead-end you will be able to dig down without any serious problems. Your long spade will be sharp enough to chop through the smaller roots with little if any delay.

If, on the other hand, you introduce your ferrets via holes from the burrow system that show, say, 10 yards (9 metres) from the tree trunk you simply drive your rabbits towards the major roots, not away from them, and can end up with a problem where thick roots prevent digging down to retrieve your ferrets. A major problem can arise when using a line ferret. There is a great risk that during its travels underground the ferret may pass either side of some of the roots and the line may become entangled. The hole may twist and turn and the ferret will do no more than tie itself to the root while simply passing along the burrow. The dead-pull reaction of your line indicates serious problems and there is no alternative to digging out, time-consuming and wasteful of time and energy though this may be. But you must make an effort since there is no way the ferret can free itself. You must try to get the ferret back.

Single bushes present no problems since the root system is likely to be small and shallow, but a thicket – a group of bushes and brambles combined – is less easy. Here the solution is to set a long net around the thicket so that it is totally surrounded and enclosed, in the hope that the rabbits can be bolted out and entangled in the net. But rabbits are always reluctant to leave cover and for that reason you may first have to clear the site with a reap-hook before line ferrets are introduced. If rabbits do become cornered and then located there are no difficulties digging down through the minor roots from the thicket.

Hedgerows, first of all, are a two-man job. You cannot work them single-handed since you cannot see both sides of the hedge at the same time. You obviously need to know what's happening on each side of the hedge. The roots from the bushes within the hedge are no real problem compared with tree roots; they can be chopped through with any sharp spade or graft. Fortunately, it is my experience that the burrows within hedgerows are generally quite small and often individual. They don't link into major systems. Thus there are no more problems to deal with than will be found in a completely open situation. It may look more difficult but it's not.

When it constructs its tunnel underground the rabbit, naturally enough, takes the line of least resistance. It therefore digs along sand and soft soil rather than scraping its way through deposits of gravel and clay. The snag here is that when the contours of the sand and soil take a sharp turn up, down, sideways or whatever the rabbit follows the same line. Thus a rabbit hole may suddenly go vertically upwards or downwards at a 90-degree angle. A rabbit can negotiate a vertical rise or fall, being able to lever and push itself up or down, using its body against the sides of the hole.

The ferret doesn't have that ability. It is a small animal in a bigger animal's home terrain. It can get no leverage from the sides of the hole since it doesn't fill that hole. The ferret may, therefore, finish up in such a fix that it can go neither forwards

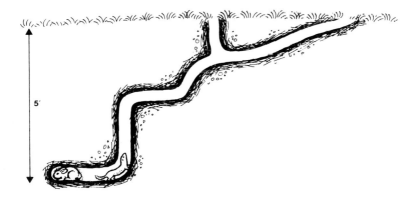

The situation in which a loose ferret may become trapped underground. It cannot climb back from a vertical drop since it lacks the body diameter of the rabbit.

nor backwards. It is well and truly stuck and you must come to its rescue with locator and spade. The ferret lacks the jumping power of the rabbit. A rabbit can jump a vertical hole 2 feet (70 centimetres) high with ease but that is impossible for the ferret.

In some situations colonies of rabbits exist in areas where they have never had the need to construct a burrow for themselves. On high ground, where there is a mixture of, say, granite and scree through years of erosion by wind, water and frost, dislodged boulders combine with the scree to accumulate a vast area of displaced rubble. There are likely to be natural gaps between the stone and the peat or thin soil and rabbits, ever opportunists, move in. This presents an extra-difficult situation for ferrets. The rabbits have many escape routes along which the ferrets cannot pass. There may be a continuing sequence of ledges, shelves and drops which the rabbit can negotiate to escape from the ferret. Terriers sometimes suffer from this same problem when they are used to evict foxes from the same sort of terrain.

The only way to dispose of these rabbits is while they are out on their feeding grounds. It is a simple matter of first locating them, recognising the best time to do the job and then dealing with them by night netting, snaring, and so on. They cannot be driven from their burrows by conventional means. Stinking out is impossible since the holes cannot be blocked, and even really drastic measures like gassing fail for that same reason. Similar problems are created both by quarrying and by natural erosion and they are also presented by the abandoned workings from open-cast mines.

The Ferreting Technique

Ferreting is the ultimate method of rabbit control since it attacks the rabbits underground. No other sporting method does that. We are able to get to rabbits in situations where they have few enemies, where they are generally safe – and they have no sanctuary if we do the work well. It isn't possible to kill every one, of course, but we can reduce their numbers to the point where crop damage is minimal. Ferreting has been perfected to the point where it does a thorough job. The ferrets force the rabbits to abandon their homes and bolt to the surface, where they can be killed by a number of methods. Or the rabbits sit tight underground as they become cornered by the ferrets. They are then either killed by the ferrets or are subsequently dug out alive.

A team of ferrets should number an absolute minimum of two and that is only sufficient if you pursue the sport only infrequently. If you are a regular, or plan to be, then because of the amount of work imposed upon them you need a minimum of four ferrets since they must not be overworked and must be rested from time to time through the day. The number of ferrets needed, though, is really governed by the size of the warrens you may be required to work and the density of the burrows within that ground.

From the functional point of view you require two types of working ferrets. There is the muzzled or loose ferret and the line ferret. It is important to be aware of which does what and why. The loose or muzzled ferret works uninterrupted and unimpeded. It is a free agent once released into a burrow and is free to go wherever it feels inclined. It is unencumbered in any way and therefore females are generally used, being smaller and less powerful than the males. On every occasion when a loose ferret is worked for rabbits it is best if it is muzzled.

The only time when this is not the case is when the ferret is introduced into an area where there are likely to be a number of rats. A muzzled ferret cannot defend itself. It is, therefore, quite helpless against a rat determined to attack. On the other hand, an unmuzzled ferret is more capable of looking after itself underground and the most powerful rats present few problems the ferret cannot master. From time to time a ferret does get bitten by a rat, usually by a female defending her young, but the clash is never fatal so far as the ferret is concerned.

At all other times, when there is no risk of an underground battle with rats, the loose ferret is muzzled. The advantage of a muzzled ferret is that it cannot kill a rabbit. It can bolt it or it can corner but so long as the muzzle is in place it cannot kill. It will frighten, scratch and force the rabbit to run.

It figures, therefore, that freed from a line controlling its movements a ferret can work much more freely and quickly – and a number of muzzled ferrets can be used within the same burrow system at the same time. Just imagine the chaos that would follow if four line ferrets were introduced together. The lines could very soon become entangled and this is a clear indication that line ferrets must only be used singly. The line ferret follows up the work begun by the loose or muzzled ferret, and is rarely if ever encumbered with a muzzle itself.

Since the loose ferret is the female, then the line ferret must be the bigger, stronger, more powerful male. He can work comfortably and easily despite the weight and restriction of the line fastened to his collar. He is restricted in the amount of travel allowed to him since most ferret lines are only 12 yards long.

The function of the line ferret is to locate those muzzled ferrets that stay below the surface once they have cornered one or more rabbits in a dead-end of a burrow. It is not essential that the male ferret is worked on a line. The function of the line is to ensure that the male animal is fully under your control. Its whereabouts is known. But this information is also readily available if the ferret is fitted with a transmitting device within its collar and the signals from this are picked up on a hand-held receiver. Some people prefer to work their male ferret on a line, saying that it gives them control over its movements. It is also possible to have locating systems fitted to all muzzled ferrets but a snag is revealed when a number are used together. For this to be effective each transmitter-receiver system needs to be based on varied signals or there is great confusion and you become unable to tell which ferret is where.

When young loose ferrets are first introduced to rabbiting I prefer to work a small burrow system and use a single ferret fitted with a transmitter. The ferret is unmuzzled. The object is to initiate the ferret to its quarry. After it has killed one or more rabbits it will have to come to terms with its duties and thereafter it is fitted with a muzzle. All my young ferrets get a similar introduction to give them the necessary experience for bigger operations within major burrow systems. For the same reason, male ferrets are introduced to the restriction of trailing a line behind them before they are given major responsibilities. This, in effect, ensures that all ferrets are ready and willing to work fully and properly and there will be no unnecessary delays or complications that could have been prevented.

So loose ferrets are released into the burrow system, one being introduced, if numbers permit, into each major entrance. They

Collar, with line attached, being fitted to a ferret.

Introducing the line ferret to a rabbit hole.

73

Line is paid out as the ferret begins its investigation.

must be allowed the necessary amount of time to do their work. They move along the underground systems to either emerge in due course or stay tight to rabbits they have encountered. In normal circumstances, where the rabbits will be first bolted and either netted or shot, the ferrets should be left undisturbed until some at least emerge and appear to lose interest. Those that vacate the burrow first should be reintroduced via other unferreted holes and this work sequence continues until all known sections of the burrow have been investigated by the animals. This stage will come to an end with some of the ferrets staying above ground while others remain underground working on rabbits they have cornered.

It can be expected that some rabbits confined in short burrows will begin to bolt quite quickly, at times almost instantly. But in bigger, longer, more complicated systems the search by the ferrets can continue for as much as 10 or even 15 minutes. Each ferreter must acquire the ability to judge the amount of time needed for loose ferrets to complete their work.

*A loose ferret emerges from a bolt-hole and should now be
reintroduced elsewhere.*

I must now draw a distinction between two types of ferreting.
There are those people whose interest is almost exclusively in
shooting bolting rabbits. I suggest that they are involved in the
sport of shooting rather than in the art of ferreting. They have no
wish to spend time digging out cornered rabbits. Those, they
would argue, cannot be shot since they will not leave their
burrow system, and so they can be left until another day, when
perhaps they will decide to bolt more readily.

My interest, though, takes ferreting all the way. My objective
– and, of course, this was one imposed upon me by my
professionalism and by the need to clear the ground of rabbits as
thoroughly as possible – was first to dispose of the bolting rabbits
and then to continue by digging out as many of the remainder as
possible. So, instead of giving up and moving on – as the man
interested only in the shooting aspect would do – I now
introduce my line ferrets in those situations where loose ferrets
remain below the ground.

In the same circumstances the shooting man would move on to

the next burrow with his remaining ferrets while keeping one eye open to watch for the emergence to the surface of any of the muzzled ferrets he had left behind. To my mind this is an untidy way of working for the shooting man doesn't make the effort to dig his ferrets out. He simply hopes they will emerge of their own accord, and this may not happen for a considerable time. To each his fun in his own way, of course, but I much prefer to use my ferrets to the full, clearing each burrow in turn as I come to it. I am not concerned with this same burrow for another day. My objective is to move on to fresh ground and not have to return to this particular patch.

I prefer to kill rabbits the easy way whenever possible, so I position a purse net over the top of every bolt-hole and every entrance, subsequently making sure that every purse net that bags a rabbit is quickly removed and replaced with a fresh net. There may be a second, or even a third rabbit about to emerge from the one hole and you must be ready to ensure that no opportunities are missed.

There are good reasons why I prefer to purse-net whenever possible rather than kill the bolting rabbits with a shotgun. First point: netted rabbits are far and away more saleable. There is no shot in them, they are undamaged and remain in first-rate condition. Shooting rabbits while ferreting is a specialist business. It is my experience that whenever I try to combine shooting and ferreting I wait a long time for the chance of a shot, then there is something else to be done. I lay the shotgun down to attend to that other chore – and, inevitably, out comes the rabbit.

If the rabbits are to be shot then the man required to do the shooting must be freed from all other responsibilities. He is the shooter; he must always be available, ready for instant action. He must not miss a chance when it comes through being preoccupied with something else. I know that a lot of youngsters gain their first experience of shooting with bolting rabbits but I do think that so much preparatory work is necessary to create the opportunity for the rabbits to be killed that the chance must not be missed. Therefore it is my view that the man with the gun needs to be an experienced and capable shot.

Long-nets are used to supplement the work of purse nets in situations where the systems are extensive and where there are a great number of bolt-holes and entrance holes. In the more complex warrens there may be as many as 100 such holes. Very few ferreters could produce 100 purse nets and the positioning and working of that number would be far too time-consuming in relation to the return from it. The alternative is to ring the complete warren system with a standing long-net. This prevents any escape across the open ground and many of the rabbits will become entangled in the net.

Long-nets have to be set properly if they are to be effective. An efficiently set long-net must contain sufficient slack to encompass the rabbits as they hit it. Were the net tight, in a way that a wire netting fence is tight, the rabbits would simply bounce off on impact and never become caught up. To make a 100-yard long-net you need 150 yards of netting. This is fastened to a top and bottom line which is 100 yards long. When the net is set the top and bottom lines are tight, but the net itself remains slack.

The standing part of the net needs to be at least 2 feet 6 inches (75 centimetres) high off the ground and here too the net needs to be slack, not taut. In my view many manufactured nets are skimped on width with the result that when they are set the necessary amount of slack within the net can only be achieved by the sacrifice of adequate height.

I like my long-nets to be 20 meshes wide and each knot spans 2 inches (5 centimetres), knot to knot. This gives adequate width to provide both the killing power and the necessary height. To catch effectively, long-nets must be set in clear, open ground. This may require the trimming back of brambles and other vegetation, and even the slashing of a narrow ride through standing vegetation with a reap-hook. The ride itself must be not less than 6 feet (1·8 metres) wide so that the rabbits run across that gap before hitting the net. They are able to run quickly and confidently across that 6-foot (1·8-metre) ride and because of their speed they become entangled. If they creep slowly forward they will not hit the net with anything like the amount of impact required to entangle them.

It is important that a long-net should be set completely clear of sticks and brambles for if these become entangled within the net it cannot function properly. Nothing is more vulnerable to tangling than loose-hanging net and great care must be taken to clear away any potential snags – and particularly in those areas where bramble, twigs, stalks and other debris have been trimmed to construct the ride in the first place.

The net can be positioned either as a box or in an approximate circle around the warren site. If the net encircles, it becomes necessary to fasten it to the top and the bottom of each of the stakes that holds the net erect. If the terrain is undulating it is also important to peg the net tight to the ground in the bottom of the hollows for otherwise rabbits will escape beneath the net. When setting a straight line of netting on level ground it is possible that one stake every 8 yards may be sufficient, but when a net is set in a circular shape the stakes will need to be closer together.

If we are tackling a very big warren it is probable that only the most likely of the bolt-holes will have been fitted with purse nets, simply because insufficient nets are available. The problem here is that while purse nets will account for all the rabbits leaving the netted holes – or those attempting to return via those holes – some rabbits will undoubtedly return to the warren via the unnetted holes. We must try to prevent this happening.

The solution is to divide the enclosed area with more standing

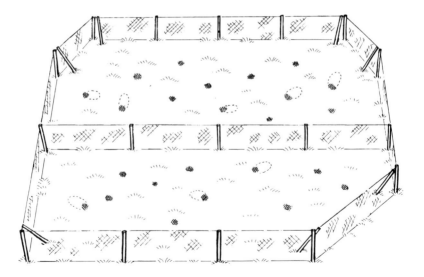

How a long-net is used to surround a warren, with one or more nets set internally to subdivide the enclosed area to restrict rabbit movements.

long-nets. Short lengths of net can be used so that ideally the enclosed space is partitioned into three sections using two nets set parallel to each other. These nets must also be fastened top and bottom to each stake since they will be required to catch rabbits bolting in either direction.

This type of long-netting is inevitably carried out in broad daylight, and the rabbits will be much more aware of the net than they are during darkness. This causes a reaction even after they have been entangled for the rabbits are inclined to bite at the net if they are left within it for too long. Ideally someone in the ferreting party will be given the task of removing each rabbit as soon as it is caught up.

Locating Rabbits Underground

Rabbits that will not bolt from a warren must be located and killed some other way. They cannot be shot or netted since they refuse to budge and will be sitting tight underground. The aim, therefore, after the bolting process has been completed, is to locate the rabbits remaining within the system wherever they may be. We know that some at least will be cornered in dead-ends by ferrets, but not all the rabbits remaining underground will have been trapped in this way. Burrow systems can be very complicated and some rabbits may never be cornered since they are able to move round and round the burrow systems – staying ahead of the ferret all the time and without the slightest inclination or pressure to leave the burrow.

We are at the stage where we need to know exactly where the remaining rabbits are, so that we can dig down to secure them. The cornered rabbits are easy. Their exact location can be determined by using the line ferret with or without a transmitter fitted to its collar. Obviously the use of a locating device makes the work easier.

In the days before locating equipment was available, I used my Norfolk long-spade to do this work. On odd occasions when there was a very strong wind or interference from farm machinery the long-spade became impracticable for listening purposes. I was therefore obliged to monitor the line ferret's progress and his approximate position by the way in which he progressed along the burrow from the moment he was introduced. It is reasonable to expect a line ferret to make a steady rather than spectacular rate of progress. The line should be gradually drawn through the handler's hands until the time when the ferret comes into close contact with a rabbit. At that stage the drawing of the line down the burrow is likely to slow, or even stop altogether. Then, suddenly, the ferret springs at the

The line ferret is in close contact with the quarry, as the line confirms.

rabbit – and something like 2 feet (60 centimetres) of line will be taken very quickly. Then, if there is no further movement, it should be obvious that the ferret has made firm contact and will be attempting to kill the rabbit.

You will be aware exactly how far the ferret has progressed down the burrow by the marking on the line attached to its collar, so you now look down the hole as the line becomes moderately tight. This should tell you roughly the direction the line is taking. Mark the spot on the surface just beyond the distance you can see down the burrow, and this is where you dig your first hole.

Take your graft – the short-handled spade with the curved blade – cut through the surface layer, whether grass or whatever, and remove it intact as a circle some 18 inches (45 centimetres) in diameter. This should be laid to the side intact so that you can restore it to its original place when the hole is refilled once the digging is completed. That way the surface area is restored and there is little sign that you have been digging underneath.

Now commence your dig, using the graft and penetrating

The first turf is lifted out intact, to be replaced later to conceal the dig.

some 2 feet (60 centimetres) with this spade. If there is a need to dig deeper, the Norfolk long-spade will be required. It may be necessary to dig down for some 3 feet (1 metre) before you break into the rabbit hole. The spoil above the hole usually caves in and you must then use the hook end of the long-spade to pick up and retrieve the ferret's line. If the hole is shallow you simply go down on hands and knees or full length, put your hand down into the hole and retrieve the line. Should there be any doubt about the direction the hole now takes it is often useful to insert a long stick up the hole. This helps you to determine the position at which your next hole should be dug. If the stick becomes obstructed that tells you that there is a diversion and you must dig at that point to determine the new direction.

So now you dig again. You clear the hole as much as may be necessary to judge the direction the line is taking within the hole, gauge where the second hole must be dug and carry on. Repeat this digging process as many times as may be necessary until you are close to the ferret. You will know exactly when this is by the

The hooked end of a Norfolk long spade is used to recover the line leading to the line ferret.

A long spade is needed for work on the deeper holes.

distance markings on your line. Once you are very close, within a foot or so, simply extend your last hole forward until the ferret is in sight. You may also be able to see the rabbit at this stage. Remove the ferret, grab the rabbit and then reintroduce the line ferret to see what happens next. There may be more rabbits down the hole and very close.

This series of moves forward along the hole is what is known as a multiple dig, but some people prefer to dig a trench all the way along the burrow until the ferret is reached. This is hard work. It involves a lot of unnecessary digging, it is time-consuming and exhausting.

The modern-day locator has everything in its favour – provided only that it is fitted with a functioning battery. This is well worth checking before every ferreting session. Most ferreters today would use one of these locators and the procedure is quite simple. Any ferret can carry the transmitting device that provides the signal to be picked up by the hand-held locator. A muzzled ferret can be used with a transmitter but this means that only one ferret can be introduced into the burrow system at any one time, unless transmitters emitting different signals are used to avoid confusion. Each ferret should have its own complete transmitter and locator system, and the signal emitted needs to differ from others that may be used at the same time.

Locator systems are very accurate indeed over a range of 6 to 7 feet (2 metres). No signal can be received outside that range but this is of no consequence. The ferret, after all, can never be very far away and the speed of the search, and the prompt response of the locating device the moment it receives a signal, makes finding the ferret quite easy. It is a matter of simply assessing the likely direction and distance the ferret may have travelled within the system to establish a starting point for the search. This done, you should work around the area you guess to be the confines of the warren system. It is unlikely that you will ever be very far away from the ferret since the area being searched is relatively small. The receiver is so powerful that it can only be a matter of a minute or two at the outside before the signal is received.

It is just a matter of working the receiver properly to ensure that the signal is received. That means working it close to the ground, sweeping it backwards and forwards through overlapping arcs. Once you have picked up a signal you concentrate in that area until the signal is received at the greatest possible volume. Then, having established a fairly exact area, the next step is to turn down the receiver volume so that you are able to pinpoint the precise spot where the receiver is immediately above the ferret. Leave the receiver on the ground in a working position as close as possible to the area where you now intend to dig and the receiver will continue to function. It can then tell you if the ferret moves away as you dig towards it. This could prevent you completing a hole which will not be necessary. If that happens simply continue the locating technique, again establish the digging point and try again, using the identical technique.

However, if the receiver continues to bleep in its working position on the ground, and no ferret has been located in the hole being dug, it can be advisable to turn the volume down to the lowest. Then hold the receiver in the hole to determine if your ferret is slightly to one side or the other. Establish that point and

The locator is worked in overlapping arcs to detect the precise whereabouts of the ferret.

The ferret's position has been determined and the dig gets under way.

The dig continues with the locator in place to advise if the ferret moves away.

it is a simple matter to enlarge the hole on that side.

Within a large warren complex it is possible for as many warreners to work independently as there is surface space for them to use. Each can have his own independent ferret on a line and each his own locator system – but each must control his own ferret carefully to ensure there is no overlapping underground. This, in effect, means that each man is working on his own section of the warren complex.

Bear in mind when buying a locator system that a working range of 6-7 feet is adequate. Longer-range devices are available on the market today but in my view they are a completely unnecessary expense. It is claimed that they have a working range of up to 15 feet (5 metres). Maybe, but there is no advantage in this whatsoever. Who wants to dig down that far?

The aim must be to make ferreting as uncomplicated as possible, but it is undeniable that complications can and do occur. It is only necessary to imagine a rabbit's reactions and its subsequent behaviour once it realises that there is an unwelcome visitor within the burrow system. I have explained how easy rabbits are to deal with in a dead-end, but a blockage can occur in the middle of a burrow when a number of rabbits have accumulated one behind the other. If the front rabbit sits tight and declines to budge there is no way the others can move.

So the ferret meets an immovable rabbit. You may well think that it is a dead-end and therefore dig down towards it. But, as you will realise, the act of digging down towards the rabbit creates a lot of disturbance and vibration. A rabbit which up to that time may have been perfectly content to sit it out suddenly has more grounds for fear. If it then moves away it allows those behind to follow suit. This can have the effect of moving the blockage further down the burrow, or it may result in one or more rabbits deciding to make a bolt for it. There is also the unwelcome possibility that as they become mobile they move into sections of the system which you were entitled to think you had already cleared.

Successful dig – both rabbit and ferret are in sight.

An enlargement of the hole reveals the ferret in action.

A blockage can also occur when two rabbits come face to face in a hole of small diameter. Neither may be prepared to give ground and the ferret, since it is unable to pass around the rabbit immediately in front of it, can do nothing. It simply scraps away at the rabbit's hindquarters but a rabbit can sit out this sort of treatment for quite long periods before feeling any need to react.

In those situations where the hole has been dug and the ferret and rabbit (or rabbits) have been located, you must be well drilled in the exact procedure to ensure that the rabbits are unable to take advantage of any opportunity you may give them to escape. A rabbit can suddenly spring forwards, upwards and away. Bear in mind that when you remove the ferret you are, in effect, taking away the rabbit's jailer. It is suddenly free of that distinctly ominous presence and sees its opportunity. Should the rabbit – even the front rabbit – already be dead, there is no problem, but at this stage you are not aware of that so you cannot afford to take any chances.

Your main safeguard is to ensure that the remaining rabbits cannot escape back into the burrow system. So you block that line of retreat by closing the route back into the system. If the hole is a shallow one, it could be as little as a few inches beneath the surface. This is an easy situation to tackle. Delve your hand as far as necessary into the dead-end and retrieve what's up there. If you cannot quite explore the full extent simply slice off another section of the hole with the spade and then reach further to complete the work.

You must take care that the rabbit is not left free to jump out and away. While its hindquarters are towards you there is no real danger, but if it turns round and you can see its head you can bet that a bid to escape is pending. Dealing with individual rabbits in these situations demands speed. Take good hold of the rabbit, pulling it from the hole, preferably by its back legs. Then, as it comes free of the hole, swiftly slide your other hand up its back to its head and quickly break its neck. The killing is instantaneous – with practice. The left hand holds the rabbit's back legs, the right hand takes hold of the rabbit's head in front of the ears. Give the head a slight turn upwards combined with a slight jerking movement and the deed is done.

The easy way – it's quick and painless.

There is no need to fear putting your hand deep into the rabbit hole. Provided your ferrets are trained and have been handled well and you have developed a good relationship with them they will not bite you. It is only when your treatment of them is lacking in some way that they are likely to show any degree of aggression. It is quite commonplace for me to thrust my hand past my ferrets, grab a rabbit by its hind legs and pull it past the ferret. Sometimes the ferret is even in the process of killing the rabbit, is hanging on by its teeth and is dragged out with the rabbit. But even this sort of treatment does not make my ferrets become aggressive.

Before dispatching the rabbit it is necessary to induce the ferret to release its hold. This is a simple procedure. Grab the ferret in the normal way of holding it, two fingers under its throat and the thumb on top of its head. Apply slight downward and backward pressure with the thumb on the top of the ferret's head, keeping the two fingers stationary, and the ferret will open its mouth. There are other ways of achieving the same result but none, I suggest, as effective as this method. I have known people to hold a rabbit down with one foot and then, after picking the ferret up in the normal way with their other hand, squeeze the ferret's foot. This obviously hurts the ferret. It opens its mouth to scream and releases its hold. It become preoccupied with its own problem and the rabbit is forgotten. But this is most unnecessary and cruel too. It goes against all of my training doctrines for fear and not trust is introduced into the relationship – to its detriment from that moment onward. The relationship is damaged. Once the ferret has released its hold on the rabbit you have still to determine whether or not there are more rabbits down the hole. If you still cannot reach up to the extreme end and determine that the burrow is now empty you must reintroduce your line ferret once more to do the job for you.

It must be borne in mind that not every dead-end of a burrow terminates in a long, narrow hole. Some are, in fact, enlarged chambers and are big enough to contain a number of rabbits. The greatest number I have ever encountered in a single dead-end is nine. I have heard of considerably larger numbers being taken by other people but when I hear such tales I am inclined to wonder how it is that so many can become so jammed together without suffocating in such a small hole.

A multiple dig, showing the sequence of digs along the burrow.

Filling in. Leaving the site neat and tidy.

Rabbits are easy to remove from a shallow burrow of the type just described but the situation is rather more difficult when the burrow is a deep one, 5 or 6 feet (1·5 to 1·8 metres) below the surface. It is then physically impossible to position yourself to be able to extend your arm down the hole to grip the rabbits. To work at this sort of depth it is necessary to dig a hole of bigger diameter and in this case you must consider your own safety.

When trying to reach down into these deep holes, especially in soft soil or sand, there is the ever-present risk of a cave-in. If you are head and shoulders into the hole a cave-in must put you very much at risk. The risk is the greater because, when you are working down that deep, in order to remove the soil from the spade the dig must be angled forward towards the rabbits. And of course you risk yourself still further by positioning yourself under an overhanging edge – you could finish up at least partially buried if there is a cave-in. Should you be working alone there is no help readily at hand and the consequences could be serious. When I was much younger I did take chances from time to time and can recall more than one close shave.

But the problem remains. Those deep-lying rabbits have still to be collected. Remove the ferret and then dig on until you can actually see the rabbit's hindquarters. The ferret is, of course, still on the line and remains close at hand on the surface near the hole. I find it convenient to control the ferret's movements by putting one foot on the line.

The next step is to remove the soil from underneath the rabbit. The rabbit then drops downwards and as soon as this happens you should reintroduce the line ferret. Now for the first time the ferret can progress beyond the rabbit and get at its head. Instead of scraping away at its hindquarters it can now kill the rabbit. Either it kills almost at once or the rabbit, realising its danger, backs towards you.

The easiest solution is to allow the ferret to complete the kill. Once the rabbit is dead it can be retrieved in your own good time. On the other hand, if it remains alive it may try to jump out of the hole and you can catch it in your hands. Sometimes the ferret simply holds the rabbit and by drawing the line you can gently move both ferret and rabbit into reaching distance. If other rabbits remain down there just repeat the process until they have all been caught. When the ferret is re-entered he will either kill another rabbit if it is there or, if it is tucked up, he will scrap away at its hindquarters. The latter will be instantly recognisable by the vibrations you can feel on the line if it is held reasonably tight. If you want to be sure of the presence of another rabbit, put more pressure on the line and the ferret will then emerge. Look at the toes of its front feet and if you discover fur on its nails you will know for sure there is another rabbit still to be captured.

Every warren is different. The appearance from the surface can be very misleading. Some are easier than they appear but many others prove much more difficult. This, in effect, means that it is impossible to predict how much time will be needed to complete the work. Moral: never start a big warren system other than at the beginning of the day's work, since you need to complete it if at all possible rather than have to extend the work into another day.

When the professional warrening was at its peak, the big estates sometimes had as many as eight men permanently employed on rabbit clearance. There were times when every man of this team would come together to work a single major warren system which might extend over as much as 50 or 60 acres. Such places still exist but even when tackling them years ago it required a full team of professionals to make any worthwhile impression on the rabbits within. That invariably meant sectioning the warren off and working it a piece at a time. Clearly the average ferreter of today could make no impression worth mentioning in that type of situation.

The point I am making here is that when you tackle a big job you need the necessary resources to complete it. In other words, instead of tackling major systems single-handed, make sure that you have some help. In some of these situations, even with the virtually unlimited manpower of years ago, the easiest solution was to work a continuous line of traps through the entrances. The population was controlled in that way instead of by ferreting. This might not have led to a massive reduction that saw the rabbits left at the lowest desirable number, but it was the best that could be done under the circumstances.

Some amateur ferreters – professionals too – are defeated by the sheer depth of a system. There is a point beyond which it becomes impracticable to continue. Assuming that you have retrieved your ferrets, reluctant though you may be to give up there is wisdom in recognising that you have reached the stage where the expenditure of more time and effort cannot be justified.

If you have been working at extreme depth and then call a halt don't block the holes up. Leave them open so that the remaining rabbits are able to escape, hopefully into other burrows or another section of the system where they will provide sport for another day. Having retrieved the ferret from these deep holes, you will have left powerful scents from the ferret within the system. The rabbits find that most objectionable and are often very pleased to leave of their own accord.

There are occasions when after a long and difficult dig, and when a long time has elapsed before the recovery of the ferret and rabbit, you may discover that your ferret has scraped at the hindquarters of the rabbit for so long that it has broken the skin, drawn blood and started to eat the rabbit before it died. This rarely happens but if the same ferret continues to do this it is advisable to discard it or use it only as a muzzled ferret.

Complications

It is impossible to predict the size of the bag for any day's work. Just as some burrow systems are easier to work than others, some contain more rabbits than others. There are also days when the rabbits are not at home. They are not underground for any of a number of reasons – or they may be underground in another burrow system altogether. It is possible to work hard at a complete system and get very little from it because of interference by other predators.

The rabbits you are after may already have been bolted by natural predators such as stoats, weasels, mink and pine martens. All of these hunt rabbits both above and below ground. In my years as a professional warrener, in the days when gin traps were permissible, I used to expect an almost daily kill of ground predators while trapping burrow systems. My twelve dozen gin traps would, in season, kill vast numbers of stoats and weasels, as well as rats and hedgehogs. It's really quite surprising how many unexpected creatures can be bolted from underground. A muzzled ferret has on a number of occasions evicted a little owl. It is probable that the owl was after beetles or insects rather than live rabbits. Little owls will kill small mammals and small birds but they do not as a rule consume the flesh direct. They are interested in the accumulation of insects that feed off carcasses. So they kill or look for carcasses already available and search them for beetles, spiders, maggots and the like, turning the bodies over from time to time to aid their search.

On occasions a feral cat will move into a burrow and have a litter down there. Stoats generally construct their own small-diameter breeding chambers underground but I have known a stoat to be evicted from burrows by ferrets. On one occasion I can even recall a bitch stoat emerging while carrying one of her brood. I can't remember ever bolting a weasel from a rabbit warren. They much prefer to do their hunting underground in mole-run systems. Weasels, in any case, very rarely tackle mature rabbits, preferring to concentrate on the very small ones and on even smaller mammals. They will, as will stoats, penetrate into a doe rabbit's breeding stop and kill her young and carry them away, perhaps to feed their own litters.

Mink are a growing problem and we cannot quite anticipate the effect they will have on the rabbit population. Their numbers are increasing annually, they are spreading wider and wider across the country and they are another predator we could manage very well without. Pine martens undoubtedly kill rabbits in hill and mountain country but that's not my scene and I cannot comment on it.

Hedgehogs have neither the speed nor the manoeuvrability to catch rabbits but I have known them to kill the young in a stop, gaining entrance during the times when the doe has left the stop unsealed just before the young rabbits are moved out. It is beyond dispute that they also account for a large number of tiny rabbits that are born in breeding chambers within burrow systems. It would be great if we could but believe the fable that hedgehogs live mainly on insects and worms and the like, but undoubtedly they destroy the nests of many ground-nesting species of birds, taking both eggs and young.

Rats will live in rabbit burrows but they usually take over one section for themselves and the rabbits leave them in isolation. They prefer not to intermingle. The rats' liking for newborn rabbits ensures they are treated with respect. Rabbits don't relish the prospect of sharing a home with rats but they are unable to move them out and must make the best of it.

Harassment over a period of time by predators entering particular warrens will undoubtedly force the rabbits to temporarily abandon their homes. Rabbits are not territorial creatures to the extent of evicting other rabbits moving into their home ground from further afield. Therefore a rabbit has no fixed abode. It will move into any refuge that happens to be conveniently available. When a predator evicts rabbits they quite happily move in elsewhere. Thus some warrens can be emptied of their stock for short periods, and particularly so while the predatory intrusions continue. It is your bad luck if the warren you choose to ferret is one of these.

Some signs of occupation can be looked for, especially after rain. Rabbit footprints and the very recent removal of fresh soil are good clues but even these are not conclusive. A predator may have scented what you see and beaten you to it by a matter of an hour or so. Alas, there can never be any certainty that your efforts will be fully rewarded.

Foxes will often enlarge rabbit burrows to make the 'earth' in which they give birth to their young. This happens annually in the February – March period, when they are actively seeking the ideal spot. From year to year foxes will traditionally use the same earths. Curiously, their tenancy is shared with rabbits remaining in other sections of the system. I have known a fox earth populated with a family of cubs while small rabbits were running around on the surface nearby.

During my time as a gamekeeper it was essential that I knew the precise location of all these extended burrows. Regular inspection enabled me to identify those showing recent signs of fox activity. While some would be used as breeding earths, others would in due course be used as hideaways as vixens brought their young from areas where they had been disturbed. Foxes have the intelligence to remain one step ahead of trouble. They know their next move and prepare for it in advance. Therefore when there is trouble afoot, they will move their young to what they regard as a more secure home. In some instances they will even transport each cub, one at a time, for as much as four miles to give them greater protection. When the young are older, able to run with her, the vixen shepherds them to their new home, induces them to move in and somehow makes sure that they are disciplined enough to stay underground in this new home even when she is not with them. In any case, she tires of their constant need for milk and leaves the earth, only returning with the necessary food to feed them.

It is not difficult to identify a rabbit burrow which has been converted to an earth and which contains fox cubs. There will be ample evidence in the form of rabbit skins and wings of all description from the food the foxes have taken to their young. In addition, the entrance will become smooth and well-trodden as the cubs emerge to play on the surface. A fox earth can be located from a considerable distance downwind by the pungent smell given off.

The fox, while an obvious danger to game birds and their young, preys mainly on rabbits. When the cubs are very small they feed quite extensively on newly born rabbits. Both dog fox and vixen will dig these out from the stops, never going in at the doe's entrance but judging the precise overhead position from which to dig down directly to the nest. They use their powerful sense of smell to locate the stops. Obviously the activity of a pair

Flash photography reveals fox cubs in part of a warren.

of adult foxes feeding a family which could number as many as eight cubs has a quite drastic effect on the local rabbit population. Yet, incredibly, young rabbits can continue to occupy another section of the same burrow system and thrive near the earth.

There must, of course, be occasions when the ferret is introduced to find another predator already in residence. I have known a ferret to bolt a fox and there are known instances of ferrets bolting foxes that have subsequently been shot. There is no doubt that a fox could kill a ferret at will but for some reason there are times when the fox prefers to flee. As recently as 1987 I was aware of a situation where a fox killed two ferrets in one burrow, a line ferret and a loose ferret. This leads me to believe the fellow concerned knew little about foxes and even less about rabbiting. There must have been a clear indication on the outside that there was a fox on the inside!

Recapturing Lost Ferrets

It is inevitable that during a series of days spent ferreting there will be one occasion or more when a loose ferret, one fitted with a muzzle, fails to return to the surface for one reason or another. Ideally, any lost ferret is best sought and recovered that same day.

A number of things might have happened underground. The most likely is that the ferret has somehow shed her muzzle and has then killed a rabbit. She may simply be sitting down there contentedly having a good meal, or sleeping one off. Obviously in such circumstances she is reluctant to leave. She may have killed a rabbit in a spot – a dead-end, for example – where it prevents her escape by blocking the burrow. Or she may be working on a rabbit and be boxed in in one direction while another ferret has backed one or more rabbits behind her. Whichever way she attempts to retreat she may have the back end of a rabbit preventing her moving either way along the hole.

She may have discovered a nest of young rabbits, a delicacy indeed in her terms, had a very good meal and then gone off to sleep within the rabbit's nest. She would find the fur within the nest warm and comfortable, reminding her of her own sleeping quarters in her hutch.

She could be trapped down a vertical hole within the burrow system. Or, of course, if she is muzzled, she may have been killed by other predators against which she would have had no defence. This is the least likely since, a fox excepted, muzzled or not she would deter most predators. Even a fox would bolt from her on occasions, but all the times I have ferreted I have never known my ferrets to bolt a fox. I suspect that is merely because I have always been able to anticipate when a fox is likely to be present as the result of scent, footprints and tell-tale evidence around the burrow mouth. Seeing that sort of evidence, I would not put a ferret into the burrow but would take other action, since the fox is a predator I can manage very well without.

The ferret is generally recognised as a powerful opponent and few other creatures would want to do battle with her. But there could be other explanations. She may have emerged from the burrow system unnoticed and either slipped away under cover or escaped into an adjoining burrow system.

Another possibility – unlikely perhaps but a possibility nonetheless – is that the terrain nearby may have been treated with rat poison, and an unmuzzled ferret can be fatally poisoned by eating a recently-poisoned rat. The only rat poison likely to have this effect is zinc phosphide. Anticoagulant poisons, poisons affecting the blood system, do not act quickly and would allow time for the ferret to resurface long before suffering any ill effects.

If the ferret is lost in a small burrow system, simply block all other holes and then place cage traps tight to the main entrances. Make a particular point of ensuring that one of these is in the hole by which the ferret entered the system in the first place. The hole must be shaped to fit very tightly around the cage trap. There must not be space for the ferret to get around the outside of the cage and remain free. If she comes out by that hole her only route must be through the cage, in which she is then recaptured. There is no need to bait the trap in any way. Traps to do this work may be purchased. Use a simple drop-ended cage, one similar to either a rat or squirrel trap or, as I do, make your own specially for the job. Cover the traps with a sack or something similar so that should the ferret emerge and be caught she is protected from the elements.

The first attempt to retrieve the lost ferret must be by the use of

Above *The cage has been positioned overnight in the burrow entrance, and the ferret has emerged.*

Right *The ferret is about to be recovered from a home-made trap.*

Shop-bought cages are also available, and these work too.

a line ferret fitted with a transmitting device. Put the line ferret through the system and the loose ferret may well be located and subsequently dug out in the same way as a rabbit. There may, of course, be one or more rabbits down there too. More usually, though, a line ferret will drive the loose ferret away and it will then come to the surface of its own accord.

If time is running short and you have neglected to bring a cage trap along with you or if you do not possess one, there is another way. Dig holes immediately in front of two or more entrance holes. These need to be 2 feet deep and 2 feet wide and straight-sided. The latter is most important. Hang rabbit intestines on a stick and string so that the intestines are positioned in the centre of the hole and just below surface level. If the ferret emerges it will try to reach the intestines and fall into the hole. That, in effect, now becomes a pit trap and because of its depth and sheer sides the ferret can neither climb nor jump out. It will remain in the pit to await your prompt attention.

Some dry leaves or grass scattered at the base of the pit will provide the ferret with some comfort. A pit of this sort is capable of catching up a ferret from either direction. If it attempts to return to the burrow system it may well become trapped on trying to get back underground. If the warren system is a really big one then the more pit traps you dig the better your chances of effecting a recovery. It helps if you drag rabbit guts on a string

101

A pit trap dug close to the entrance with a bait positioned to lure the ferret.

around the surface of the burrow in the direction of the bait hung within the trap. This creates a scent trail and increases the trap's effectiveness.

If the ferret has fallen down a vertical hole within the burrow the line ferret, on approaching, may not necessarily do the same thing. It is just as likely to draw back from the hole. Ferrets are reluctant to enter a vertical shaft – which explains why ferrets very rarely enter bolt-holes that drop down vertically from the surface. If that is the case then you have real problems. There is only one potential solution. You have no transmitter on the loose ferret so the only possible means of location has to be via that Norfolk long-spade – used as a listening device. I can do that, probably a number of other people can do it too, but the vast majority wouldn't have the remotest idea what to listen for or know how it is done. Many have never even seen a Norfolk long-spade and many others have become too reliant upon the locator.

Give yourself a few lessons at the first opportunity. Wait until a ferret fitted with a transmitter has taken up a fixed position

Success! The ferret is in the pit and it cannot escape.

down a burrow. Establish exactly where it is with the aid of the locator system . . . and then introduce your Norfolk long-spade. Push the blade 10 or 12 inches (25 or 30 centimetres) into the ground immediately above the exact position of the ferret as defined by the locator and then put your ear to the ash shaft of the long-spade. No other part of your body nor any part of your clothing should touch the spade – only your ear. Everyone at the site must stand still.

Listening to rabbit/ferret activity underground with the Norfolk long spade.

Now listen. You should get a good signal right away. The handle of the spade transmits the vibrations of the ferret – perhaps it is working on a rabbit – direct to your ear. You become aware of the ferret scraping at the rabbit, or of it killing the rabbit, or of the rabbit thumping in the hole. Keep listening until you are sure that you will recognise the sounds the next time you hear them, then withdraw the spade and push it back into the ground some feet away. Listen again. You will still hear the same commotion (assuming it is still going on) but much more faintly. Keep trying different spots until you become aware of how and where to obtain the best signal. Once you can do this without the aid of the locator, you will have the satisfaction of knowing that your own skills alone will enable you to make use of this last-ditch method of rescue.

If your muzzled ferret is lost in thick undergrowth on the surface the same recapture methods apply – the pit trap will do the job for you. Keep very quiet on approaching the area to be searched. Listen for the sound of birds becoming agitated. Blackbirds, wrens and some others will mock a ferret just as readily as they mock any other predator.

With luck you may effect a recapture the same day by one or other of the methods described. However, you may not always be so lucky and it may be necessary to return to the site the next day. In fact you must look in there three times every day until the ferret is retrieved. The longer the lapse of time the less your chance of success, but ferrets can live for a considerable period within a burrow system – as much as three weeks. This is especially so if they have lost their muzzles, for it is likely they will have all the food they require down there with them. Then they are most likely to be forced to the surface by lack of water. If your ferret continues to fail to reappear another possibility must be considered – that someone else passing by has recovered it for you!

A good trained dog can be of value in these circumstances. If allowed to roam around the surface above the burrow it can often detect the whereabouts of a ferret or rabbits by scent and hearing. If the dog's interest centres upon a particular section, that is where you should concentrate your own efforts.

The lesson of all this must be never to lose a ferret in the first place. But that's easier said than done, and you will be lucky indeed if it never happens to you. But should your ferret escape, become hungry and – once its muzzle has rotted through – enjoy itself in someone else's hen roost, there is no way that you can claim it back. It couldn't possibly have been yours after all, now could it?

Ferreting with Dogs and Guns

While my preferred method is to use long-nets to surround the warrens and catch the bulk of the rabbits that way, I recognise that there are others who prefer to shoot instead of net. Shooting can be effective and sporting too, but I think it vital that everyone who shoots in these situations should be a very capable gun and able to kill a very large proportion of what he fires at. One snag, of course, is that this is unlike shooting over truly open ground. The rabbits are in and out of vision and quickly back down another hole if the opportunity is there. This also applies to rabbits that may be injured. There are escape routes for those, too, and if injured rabbits do get back into the system they are likely to be extremely difficult to capture.

When loose ferrets become involved in the eviction of wounded or dying rabbits the rabbits will not bolt a second time even if they are able. If the loose ferrets make contact with the wounded rabbits they become preoccupied, stay where they are and do not resurface. This wastes valuable time.

It is important that whenever a rabbit is shot at it should be well clear of the hole. Sometimes a rabbit can be shot in a burrow entrance but, even if such a shot is successful and the rabbit is killed, there is a strong possibility that with its last few movements the rabbit will kick its way far enough down the burrow to make capture difficult. And, of course, if the enthusiastic shooter fires at a rabbit in a burrow entrance there is some risk of killing an unseen ferret just behind it.

The safety aspect must be given every consideration. If the warren system is a big one it may require two guns to do the killing. For their own safety they should stand back to back so that they have a completely free field of fire over 180 degrees each. Anyone else should get out of range. Where the burrows are located in a bank it is necessary for the gun to stand on the

Young gun in position to take bolting rabbits.

bank to see both sides. A hedge with its vegetation preventing all-round vision requires one gun on each side of it – and each man needs to know exactly where the other man is standing. Neither should move without informing the other.

If the burrow is a small one in flat territory, one man can effectively do all the shooting required and will stand in the middle, shooting round the full 360 degrees. If there are two guns they should stand side by side on the edge of the burrow, one shooting to the right and the other to the left, so that neither is endangered by whatever the other fellow does. This sort of discipline is essential. Shooting must never be haphazard or the consequences can be very serious indeed. To prevent accidents the guns should never be loaded until the ferrets are introduced to the burrows. Until that time guns should remain broken. It follows, of course, that each time a gun is laid down it must first be broken and unloaded.

If two people are shooting and both decide that there will be no more rabbits bolting then both should finish shooting together. It can be dangerous for one to stay with his gun while the other returns to the task of retrieving the ferrets that may have emerged in the meantime. This is snap shooting at its best. There may be only brief glimpses of the rabbit and it must be shot quickly and accurately or the opportunity is lost. The rabbits, having been bolted, will be moving at reasonable speed over a short distance. Everyone enjoys himself as he thinks fit, and I acknowledge the fun of shooting. But I have also come to realise that standing as still as you must while waiting for your chance to come on a frosty day is not exactly the height of pleasure. Shoot your rabbits if you will; give me that net.

For so long as I can recall I have always had kennels and an assortment of dogs to help me in my work. I have never had fewer than three and often four dogs, since there is a use for a variety of species within the wide aspect of shooting and the countryside. Over the years this has averaged out at two gundogs and two rabbiting dogs. The gundogs were primarily for picking up at pheasant shoots and for work on my own shoot, but one of them, a Springer spaniel, was also used for hunting out rough-lying rabbits and also for retrieving shot rabbits from difficult situations. The other two were a lurcher and a terrier. These were both essentially rabbiting dogs but the terrier really served a dual purpose thanks to a commitment to ground vermin. The terrier, a Jack Russell, was always a hunting animal, working rough ground and even going to ground in those situations where it could safely get down into a fox earth or a drainpipe. I prefer a broken coated terrier. Jack Russell terriers are mostly white with variable colour markings. This is most helpful, as they can be seen easily when hunting. Some will give tongue when on the scent of a rabbit and this helps to determine their position and keeps rabbits on the move.

From a ferreting viewpoint the Jack Russell was used on the warren. These dogs have good hearing and scenting ability and are able to locate rabbits and ferrets and indeed any commotion that occurs underground. Not only does a Jack Russell give a good indication of the whereabouts of ferrets and rabbits underground but it saves time, giving an accurate indication of where to begin sweeping the ground with a locator. Jack Russells are difficult animals to teach to retrieve – I have only had one that would do it properly – but they can be taught to work nets, drive rabbits into nets and to be thoroughly disciplined in all they do.

These dogs are absolutely fearless and will tackle anything from a weasel to a fox without a second thought. Ratting is second nature to a Jack Russell and through constant practice they learn the difference between a rabbit and vermin, knowing which they should kill and which they simply hold.

The bag-filler was the lurcher. These dogs are very intelligent and relatively easy to train. Mine were always the breed of Norfolk lurcher, a cross between a Smithfield and a greyhound. A Smithfield is a leggy type of collie of the sort that bullock drovers used when working cattle half a century ago. A lurcher is not a defined breed. There are any number of cross species that can combine to produce a lurcher but in my view the best of all is the Norfolk lurcher. It combines the brains of the collie with the speed of the greyhound, which makes it an animal ideally suited for chase-and-catch situations. It has the speed, the stamina and the ability to think as it moves in for the kill and needs to out-think a twisting and turning rabbit.

In recent years lurchers have come back very strongly to be very popular animals. Deerhound and Saluki crosses are one popular arrival but these, in my view, are too big for the work I want from my lurcher. They cannot get around so nimbly in scrub vegetation as the Norfolk lurcher; they are really for coursing, for a long chase after hares, and my animals are not used for that. Neither, I believe, are they so easy to train, and I suggest that they lack the brain power of the Norfolk.

A litter of lurchers will provide a cross-section of the species. Some will be smooth-coated, after the greyhound, while others will be rough-coated, after the collie. My own preference has always been for the rough coated variety since these can withstand weather and rough going very much better. They must be taught to retrieve but mine have always been intelligent enough to quickly acquire the knack after limited training.

If the training starts at a young enough age, when the animal is still a puppy, it all comes naturally. All my work has been involved with estates where game birds were the prime consideration. With that in mind, it was always essential that my lurchers were trained not to interfere with pheasants and partridges. There is no difficulty in teaching the Norfolk lurcher this distinction. It is every bit as easy as teaching it that chickens, ducks, turkeys and sheep are taboo.

The poaching fraternity has other uses for the lurcher. Whereas I teach my dogs to disregard game birds and deer, the lurcher is very competent at acquiring the skills of poaching and is usually the animal to accompany deer and game-stealing gangs wherever they operate.

Lurchers are, in fact, very versatile animals. They can go to work when about one year old and have a working life up to the age of approximately ten years. A lurcher has all the necessary speed to catch and seize any speeding rabbit or even hare, but in truth virtually any dog that's half a dog can catch a bolting rabbit during ferreting. The rabbit runs to a hole you have already ferreted and blocked up and is immediately mesmerised and doesn't know where to go next. It is easy prey – I've caught them myself.

As highly trained animals, the dogs do not need to be restrained at the warren site. They are left to their own devices, to do as they please, and they will do everything required of them without instruction. They will leave a netted rabbit as they will have been trained to do but give full chase to those running free. They are so keen to get on with it that they can be guaranteed to see the rabbit before any human and are fast off the mark. They are constantly alert and need no urging. In fact, when you are working small burrow systems a dog can generally tell you if a rabbit is at home.

The Influence of the Weather

As with all outdoor activities, the weather plays a big part in the success or otherwise of ferreting for rabbits. The weather influences the actual location of the rabbits and it helps determine whether they are underground or on the surface. So many variables play a part – sunlight, wind, rain, snow and frost all affecting ferreting in one way or another. Some are beneficial for some aspects of rabbiting, detrimental to others. But let us look at the weather's influence on ferreting.

Rain has an obvious effect in two ways. It makes the actual work of ferreting uncomfortable and those days when the rainfall is persistent are neither comfortable nor the most sporting. They are to be avoided if possible. But it must be equally obvious that during spells of prolonged rain the rabbits are much more likely to stay underground in the warmth and security of their burrow systems rather than braving it out in the open and being constantly soaked.

Rain is hard on your hands during ferreting, nets become unmanageable and less effective and it isn't possible either to kneel or lie on the ground in any comfort. Without doubt dry days make for better ferreting but, on the other hand, there will be more rabbits underground during wet weather. It seems that their food intake is reduced because of this preference for staying warm and dry and neither do they travel so far for their food. Intake is spasmodic. They move out, quickly consume what they need and are soon back below ground with the minimum of delay. But, if the prospects are therefore better in that respect, no one shoots as well, no one works as well, everyone is uncomfortable, and dogs look wet, cold and miserable and become disinterested. So far as I am concerned, wet-weather ferreting isn't worth the effort.

Wind has the effect of moving rabbits out of those burrows that are fully exposed. They become draughty and cold. Rabbits find them uncomfortable and they move out to warmer quarters. So during windy days you do better working burrows with entrances unaffected by wind. These will remain warm and will be the places other rabbits displaced from less comfortable quarters move into. Therefore such burrows give you a greater return for the effort expended. An advantage of wind is that it at least partially kills sound. This means that, especially when working hedgerows, if you begin downwind and work upwind, the rabbits are less likely to have been forewarned. The noise factor is reduced.

If the wind is strong it bellies your long-net, thus reducing its catching potential. The net bellies out and, if the quarry is running into it downwind, the net can be blown off the rabbit. Where the net should be very slack it becomes much tighter. Another, and perhaps the worst aspect is that the wind has the habit of blowing debris into the net so that it becomes entangled and this too limits its catching ability.

It is perfectly possible to catch rabbits while ferreting with snow lying on the ground, but I do think that snow makes long-netting impossible as the net becomes clogged, wet and inoperable. Purse nets remain unaffected and are as functional as at any other time. So if you do ferret with snow on the ground I recommend that you use purse nets only. It is, though, well worth remembering that snow may cover over some of the bolt-holes, maybe even entrances too, so that some become difficult to locate whereas others will be plain to see. You may think you have purse-netted every hole only for a bolting rabbit suddenly to push up through the snow as if from nowhere and make its bid to escape. This is where dogs come into their own for they are not hampered so much as the rabbits and the odds are shortened in favour of the dog in every chase. The rabbits are much more likely to be below ground after a snowfall, since they become very much more vulnerable on the surface with their cover blotted out and their feeding areas restricted.

The only notable effect of frost on ferreting is on the digging, and then only if the frost is prolonged and severe. Frost also influences netting with both purse and long-nets since it becomes very much more difficult to peg the nets to the ground. As a matter of personal preference, during prolonged hard and frosty weather I would be inclined to limit my ferreting activity to shooting the bolting rabbits, leaving the digging out to the barest minimum. Frosted ground is hard on dogs' feet and legs and is also dangerous for them. They too risk broken limbs.

Sunny days are pleasant days, especially if there is only a modest breeze. All equipment should work perfectly and dogs, ferrets and humans are all in good heart. But sunny days and shooting can combine to cause complications. There is no fun at all in repeatedly looking into bright sunlight, straining your eyes and wondering all the time what's happening – because it is almost certain that you will be unable to see as well as you really need to. During sunny days in the ferreting season the sun is low in the sky and that makes the situation even worse. Guns with their backs towards the sun have no problems, of course, so this factor must be taken into account when the guns are positioned.

Sunshine on snow affects all shooters whatever position they take up, because the sun and snow together produce glare and this is very trying on the eyes – especially at ground level.

Fog curtails shooting because of the danger but has no other effect on operations. Foggy days are usually still days and are beneficial in that they do help you to hear what's happening underground – but they are not so helpful from the point of view of disturbance.

I am often asked what makes a good day for bolting rabbits, bearing in mind that on some occasions they will readily leave the ground regardless of surface conditions, whereas at other times – often under what appear to be favourable conditions – they just cannot be budged. I am still searching for the answer to that one. To date I must admit that I don't know why they sit tight. If they are already nervous – if, for example, a predator has recently been harassing them underground – they may be less inclined to endure further stress and make a bolt for it as soon as the ferret shows itself. But we must, I suppose, acknowledge that rabbits, like us, are living creatures and not always predictable.

Warren Repopulation

Once a major effort has been completed against either a warren or a burrow system it can be expected that the area has been fairly well cleared. With any luck, the majority of the rabbits will have been killed and, if everything went well and there were no snags, the population could have been very substantially reduced. Once all work on the system has been completed, then the ground must be tidied up and left in such a state that it is easy to assess at a later date what rabbits have been left behind.

So all the excavations are filled in for the sake of tidiness, and all the bolt-holes and entrance holes are filled in to help assess what's been left. The surviving rabbits will emerge from the system, digging their way out through favoured holes almost overnight. Since they have been disturbed and more than a little frightened in the process they will vacate the burrow, will very likely feed and then either lie rough on the surface somewhere or go to ground in a completely fresh burrow system.

If the warren and burrow systems are first cleared in the autumn, subsequent work in the area on other systems is likely to lead to rabbits evicted from one set of burrows going to ground elsewhere. This then inevitably means that by the early spring it is worth working the same ground a second time. As a professional I always work the same ground in two separate operations. The area is given time to restabilise and the rabbits time to come to terms with the changed situation. As a result, the second visit sees a number of entrances and bolt-holes still closed up while the remainder are back in use. This makes the second ferreting campaign very much easier since there are fewer holes to deal with. This can, in effect, mean that purse nets can do the whole of the killing work and there may be no need of a long-net.

It pays to do the first work well, of course, for if there are frequent digging-out excavations you, in effect, sever the burrow systems and then fill them in. Thus a number of sections become cut off from the entrances and these might well not be reopened. Therefore, on the second occasion you find the rabbits occupying a restricted section of the system. On the other hand, if no digging out and filling in is done first time, the remaining rabbits retain a free run of the entire system and are much more difficult to corner.

After the second operation all the reopened holes and diggings are filled in as before. If you have been very lucky and efficient you may have reduced the area stock to a very low level. But with rabbits nothing is stabilised for very long. More rabbits are likely to move in, more rabbits are bred and no area stays denuded for very long.

Rabbits are great travellers. I know that from my own experience and I can prove it by reference to an occasion when an area of big fruit trees was sprayed with lime sulphur, a winter spray. This discoloured the vegetation under the trees and the resident rabbits quickly acquired that colouring on their feet and their fur. Within a matter of days some were caught more than half a mile away. I recall the situation all the more clearly because, when I tried to market those rabbits, the dealer thought there was something wrong with them. As a matter of interest, a similarly-affected hedgehog showed up three fields away overnight.

You may have done a good job on your own patch but you cannot clear the entire neighbourhood. Eventually, no matter how much you and even neighbours clear, there will be big colonies of rabbits left unculled. These infiltrate back and spread through the cleared area to repopulate the ground. This inevitably means that there is a sufficient breeding stock around to continue the cycle – and there will be a good supply of rabbits available for next year. Fortunately, it seems never-ending!

When the rabbit stock was reduced by myxomatosis to less than one per cent of what it had been, a number of warren systems inevitably became untenanted. So, being unused, they progressively deteriorated and caved in and the entrances filled in or became overgrown with vegetation. To all outward appearances the warren systems became non-existent. Some were even cultivated over and their long-time entrances completely disappeared. For two or three years there were few if any signs that rabbits survived. Yet slowly but surely they came back.

As their numbers grew so they spread out from the areas still occupied and the abandoned warrens slowly began to be reoccupied. Even where the entrances were very well hidden by ploughing and cultivation, the rabbits somehow found their way back to the selfsame underground burrows their predecessors had used for generations. And they are still there now. It is one of those inexplicable events that a rabbit hole in the middle of a field can be gassed and its population exterminated, the hole filled in and cultivated over the top, yet, even after the passage of a number of years, a rabbit will go to that exact location and restore the old system.

6
Day and Night Long-Netting

We live in changing times. Recreation has changed. Freed from the need to work quite so hard to survive, man has been able to change some of his long-term habits. Television in every home may be a blessing for the old and infirm, indeed for all of us at times, but that, the motor car, foreign travel and umpteen other things have all combined to affect attitudes towards sport and leisure. There is no longer the mass interest in football there used to be. And it must be said that while there has been a greater interest in ferreting and in the shooting side of rabbiting the netting interest has declined.

I regret that this is so. Netting has many advantages for those who do it well, who choose the right time, place, wind and situation. It is a sport, at least in my view, although I acknowledge there is a great deal of hard work involved both on the actual occasion and in the preparation. This work must be well organised and error-free on the night or the result will be total failure.

It is now most unusual for me to find anyone with whom I can have a knowledgeable chat about day and night netting. The skill is in some danger of being lost, but I insist that there is so much fun and pleasure in it and the methods are so effective that it should never be allowed to die out. Years ago, in fact, in the days before television, I was frequently asked 'Are you going netting? Can I come with you?' by people who were keen to see what happened and who were prepared to treat it as a spectator sport. Nowadays the public attitude is much more likely to be: I must be in the house at 10.30 to watch *Sports Report* or whatever.

I suppose it is a spectator sport of a sort but from the operator's viewpoint the presence of uninitiated onlookers has a great number of debit points. I am used to working after dark. I have, as have other people in similar situations, developed the ability to almost see in the dark. This is an acquired skill which develops over a long period. As a result I can, for example, see my standing net on the darkest night and won't therefore trip over it. I can't say that for spectators! It is probably a fact that few people have ever thought about, but a fact nonetheless, that nights are not so dark now as they used to be. Most villages have some form of street lighting and the lights of major towns are reflected by the clouds and their effect is extended by many miles. The average man may perhaps think it an exaggeration but I do assure you that this is factually so and nights are not now so dark that I cannot be completely aware of what is happening around me before, during and after the nets have been set.

There is no reason why netting should be allowed to die out. The cost of the net is really only minimal, the method is humane, it is extremely effective and can dispose of rabbits living in situations in which all other methods either fail totally or are far less effective. It can take large numbers of rabbits that live above the ground in dense woodland and it can do that same job in wooded areas where ferreting is not allowed because of other interests. It can crop areas of marshland and it allows you to kill your neighbours' rabbits when they come on to your land to feed. Remember that when a rabbit comes through your boundary fence onto your land it automatically changes ownership. It is your property if you can kill it.

Night netting can be carried out after dark around well stocked game coverts with only minimal disturbance to the birds in places where both shooting and ferreting the rabbits would be far more of an interference. So it is possible to kill large numbers of rabbits that are doing a massive amount of crop damage by this method and by no other. Therefore I firmly believe that there is a place for netting on into the future. But it continues to lose popularity – for all the wrong reasons.

There is nothing really difficult about it. Once you or anyone else understands exactly what's required it is very easy. A 100-yard net can be properly set in less than five minutes – I could do that single-handed out of experience, but there is nothing in the technique that any novice need regard as prohibitive. He will have his failures, of course, but there will always be failures while learning anything and I can only repeat that it is a method well worth learning.

Bear in mind as the starting-point that your permission to use someone's land for rabbiting may very well not extend to after-dark activities, so ensure that this point is clarified. Make sure that both the farmer and the gamekeeper approve – and ensure that they know the exact date, time and place of your intended nettings. Poachers operate after dark and it is crucial that you should not be confused with them, unwittingly provide them with cover, or create any confusion which might result in their not being apprehended.

Rabbits can be netted all the year round. The main time may well be from harvest through to April the following year, but netting is in fact selective because the size of the mesh allows small rabbits to escape – to be netted some other time when they have grown bigger. The difficulty of netting in summer and early autumn relates to the problems of pushing the net stakes into the ground easily. Obviously this needs to be done without undue pressure; hammering is out of the question, and the stakes must not be broken.

Hazel stakes are unquestionably the best but when I caught rabbits professionally I had the estate make me up a set of iron stakes of only $\frac{3}{8}$ inch (1 centimetre) diameter, with a small shoulder at the top to prevent the top line sliding down the stake. These were an improvement during dry weather conditions since the metal penetrated the ground much more easily than the wood, but there were disadvantages too. They were heavier and more noisy than wood – and quite hard on the tummy when they were pushed into the ground.

Night netting requires that your nets are set between the rabbits' home ground and their feeding areas. Your net intercepts them when they return from feeding and you must therefore ensure that the nets are set in exactly the right place – without the rabbits being aware of your presence. Quietness is the name of the game.

It is essential that both wind strength and direction serve your purpose. The wind must be blowing from them to you, since this not only minimises the noise you may inadvertently make but it prevents your scent blowing towards the rabbits and giving them advance warning that all's not well. This is an absolute necessity and to work in defiance of it means total failure.

A short tag of tape on the top line of your long-net tells you top from bottom in the dark.

It can be fast work setting a long-net if the stakes are ready to hand.

119

Above *A support stake is used to take the stress when the long-net deviates from a straight line.*

Right *A close-up of the method by which the top line is secured to the stakes.*

Moonlit nights are to be avoided. I have had good catches before the moon rises and have also done well after it has set, but periods when the moon is bright at night are best ignored. However, it is pointless to plan too far ahead. You can really only make your decision to go netting in a particular area that same day. A wind from a direction that makes netting impossible in one area may be ideal somewhere else and it is, therefore, important that you should have surveyed your terrain with great care so that you are well aware of this.

Wind can be powerful. Anything over Force 5 is prohibitive, and ideally the wind will be light to moderate. Some wind is helpful, but too much is destructive. It blows debris into the net and it tightens the net rather like wire netting and decreases its catching power.

Successful netting is about getting all the details right. The starting point is really what you wear on the night. Netting can catch up in virtually everything. I have already explained how debris such as brambles impairs a net's efficiency. Realise also that what you wear affects your efficiency. Avoid wearing any outside clothing fitted with buttons or buckles. This applies particularly to your coat. My own solution is to wear a one-piece smock that fits over my head. It is the type that sea fishermen use for exactly the same reason. If you must wear a jacket, cut the buttons off and fasten it with string through the button holes. Rubber boots are fine provided they have no buckle-and-strap fasteners just below the knee. A good tight-fitting cap or hat is useful since there is nothing worse than groping about in the dark to recover a wind-blown hat.

Reconnaissance

The survey in advance of the netting serves a number of purposes. You need to know the precise location of every gate and the way each gate opens. You need to be able to move through each one easily, without confusion or noise. Vehicles must be left some distance away from the netting site, and downwind too, so find yourself a convenient parking site during daylight for use after dark.

The survey should also tell you the whereabouts of cattle and other farm animals. In no circumstances can you set your net on a field inhabited by any farm animals, for these can panic and run into the standing nets –not only destroying the evening's sport but also destroying the nets. It matters not if there are farm animals on the area in which the rabbits will be feeding and from which the rabbits will later be driven. So long as the animals cannot make contact with the nets there is no problem.

The real purpose of the survey is to establish the exact feeding grounds of the rabbits. These may be close at hand, perhaps even in the very field where you will set your net, or they may be two or even three fields away. Again there is the possibility that they can be spread over three fields rather than concentrated into one. You discover where the rabbits are by looking for their work. There will be recent traces of rabbit occupation in runs across to the feeding areas and through any hedges that may intervene. There must, of course, be something fairly obvious for them to feed on. They cannot feed on ploughed land for there's nothing there. So look for areas where root crops have been harvested but where the green tops remain, pastures, and indeed anywhere where green food is evident.

The Netting Operation

With your preparation and your prospecting complete it then becomes a simple matter of erecting the net in the right place on the night. Bear in mind that rabbits always net better when they are running downhill, so take advantage of that if possible. All rabbits flushed from open land are fully exposed. They panic when driven out into the open and their first thought is to find cover as quickly as they can. So they pick up full speed and run for cover – and your net should be carefully positioned so they hit it just before reaching safety. They become entangled in such a way that it is very rare for any to wriggle free, and while there is ample time to collect them at relative leisure they should nonetheless be collected as quickly as possible.

Ideally the netting team should consist of three people. The first runs the nets out, keeping them reasonably tight. The second person carries the stakes and hands them to the third, unpointed ends first, who then pushes them into the ground and fastens the top line to the net with a half-hitch. It is easiest if the man carrying the stake walks behind the net and the man setting the net walks in front of it. Get them set quickly and efficiently. One person must remain at the nets all the time to deal with the rabbits as they become entangled.

The other two become beaters once the net is set. They must walk into position behind the rabbits without disturbing them in any way. They then either flush the rabbits by tapping two sticks together or by dragging a long line between them across the field or fields towards the net. Using a line disturbs all the rabbits; it touches them and they then dash for home.

It is easiest to extricate rabbits from the nets if you kill them first. This prevents the rabbits from struggling and from getting further entangled in the netting. I have my own method here too. I always position myself on the side in which the rabbits hit the net. I walk up to the spot where a rabbit is entangled, I get down on one knee and lift the top line of the net over the back of my head. The net is thus supported and I then push the sideways slackness of the net in either direction from me with a movement of either hand. It is then so much easier to remove the rabbit since the possibility of further tangling is virtually eliminated.

When the rabbits are removed from the net I always toss mine belly upwards to the ground so that the white hair on the underside makes the rabbit more visible in the darkness and I can then collect it later once the killing operation has been completed all along the net.

Once the operation is complete you now come to the next stage – and this depends on whether or not the same nets are to be used again that night. If not, the nets can be collected quickly and without too much care, to be cleared of any debris, maybe dried and even repaired the next day. On the other hand it may well be that you plan to reset the nets somewhere else and net again that same night. In that case the net must be gathered up with extreme care, since care taken now will mean the net can be set that much more easily at the next site.

The procedure is as follows. One man collects the stakes, never getting more than one stake ahead of the man who will pick up the net. Some people gather their nets directly on to a stake. I prefer to gather mine on my fingers until they are full, and then transfer it onto the iron stake positioned at the end of the net and

A rabbit being removed during night netting. Note that the net's top line runs across the back of the head to take up the slack.

The work needs to be fast and systematic.

The rabbit is thrown down white belly upwards to make it more visible during collection later.

A good average return from one set of the net.

124

held in the crook of my left arm. This ensures that the net remains twist-free and that odd pieces of debris, twigs or whatever, can be removed as you progress.

Difficulties and Surprises

It is not always plain sailing. There are difficulties which may need to be overcome. The conditions may be perfect from the weather point of view, the nets may be set efficiently and quickly but rabbits are almost non-existent. For instance, the ground you are netting may have been worked by a fox, cat or dog just before your arrival on the scene and the rabbits sent scurrying for home. Poachers could have been there before you and creamed off some of the rabbits, or there may have been a more innocent intrusion by a courting couple on the site. One way of combating illicit netting is to lay a number of thorn twigs across the netting area. This will make the operations of poachers that much more difficult, or even force them to pack it in altogether. All you need to do is to collect the thorns yourself the day before your own net is set – and this is easy enough since you know precisely where they are. Intrusion by poachers was much more prevalent years ago than it is now. During my term in Derbyshire a lot of rabbit netting was carried out and the thorn defence was very necessary. I have even known poachers remove the thorns themselves in the afternoon of their own planned expedition.

If you are netting alone – I have done this lots of times – you cannot work more than 150 – 175 yards (135 – 160 metres) of nets, whereas a team can set several hundreds of yards. This amount of netting, plus the stakes, net bags and resulting catch, is as much as one individual can sensibly cope with. When working alone, I carry my stakes in a sack over my left shoulder. I run the nets out to the full extent and erect them on the return journey. When working single-handed there is no one available to beat the ground in front of the net to send the rabbits running for home. In these circumstances I use a dog, either a Jack Russell or a lurcher. Both can be trained to work to the net in the dark. They chase individual rabbits into the net, then return to the feeding ground and continue as before, until they have chased all the rabbits off. If the lurcher catches a rabbit on the feeding grounds it will almost invariably scream – and this is the best thing to happen. It immediately alarms all the others and they head for home at speed.

From time to time it is inevitable there will be some unwelcome arrivals in the net. I have caught up cats and hedgehogs – with the latter by far the most unwelcome. A hedgehog tries to climb up the net and when it hears you approach it promptly rolls up into a ball. No prizes for guessing what happens to the net – and you are left with the task of extricating the hedgehog without damaging the net or wasting too much time. The spines become fully extended and if you confuse a hedgehog with a rabbit and make a hasty grab at it you will have cause for regret. The nets will catch the occasional hare but these present no problems, becoming entangled in exactly the same manner as rabbits.

Night netting is by far the most successful aspect of all long-netting, but that does not mean that rabbits cannot in some circumstances be netted in broad daylight. I have already explained the use of long-nets while ferreting, but long-nets can also be set with advantage on rough pasture ground. As before the nets are set in front of the warren systems. If numbers of rabbits are sitting out within this rough ground they can be totally enclosed if sufficient nets are available. When working alone, or perhaps with a dog, you can flush the rabbits from their seats. Being totally exposed, the rabbits hightail it for home and, broad daylight or not, run headlong into the nets. They are caught very well since they are travelling at top speed.

Netting – and Poaching – on a Derbyshire Estate

A morning set provides another good opportunity. Given the right type of territory this can be most successful. I have already mentioned that I worked in Derbyshire. I was based on a big estate where there were extensive herds of grazing cattle. The estate had two large areas of parkland. South Park, containing a herd of fallow deer, was surrounded by an 8 foot (2·5-metre) deer fence; North Park was divided into areas for cattle grazing by iron fencing and barbed wire. A huge wood marked the boundary on one side. The main Derby – Chesterfield road ran

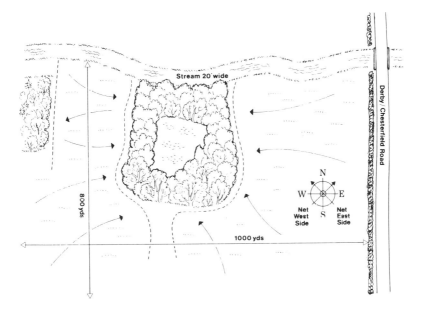

Layout of a real-life early morning long-netting situation. The dotted lines indicate the setting position for the nets.

along the other flank and this was fenced off with rabbit-proof wire netting and was screened from the road by a long, narrow spinney. On the extreme northern end of the park a stream some 20 feet (6 metres) wide acted as a rabbit barrier along that side.

As a result of subsidence, the ground was one mass of hillocks and hollows, extending in all over some 70 acres. A few mature oaks were scattered here and there. The wood was mostly of hardwood – oaks, beeches and elms – with an occasional small clump of conifers undergrown by a mass of rhododendron. A good habitat for rabbits, and it held a large number.

The method of netting was to set nets the full length of the wood from the stream, some 500 yards (450 metres) or so. This was a three-man operation, as for night netting. The only real difference was that when the weather was favourable we arrived at the site one hour before dawn to set the nets. All we had to do was to patrol up and down the nets, take out the rabbits and wait for daylight. The rabbits mostly came in of their own accord. The

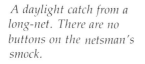

A daylight catch from a long-net. There are no buttons on the netsman's smock.

few that remained squatted out in the open or tucked themselves into tiny holes, often with their hindquarters clearly visible. These rabbits were easily disposed of. The few burrows in this immediate area had never been allowed to develop fully. They were closed down from time to time and checked the day prior to our morning operation. All the rabbits lived in the wood.

These morning sets would be begun at the time when enough of the young rabbits were big enough to sell. The income funded not only the keeper's wages but also those of the pit bobby – the estate policeman. Small rabbits passed through the nets and would escape for another day. The does would be bagged unharmed and transferred to another part of the estate to supplement breeding stocks in natural and man-made warrens kept exclusively for sport shooting. The three-quarter grown rabbits and mature bucks were culled and sold.

When we netted the other side of the wood we had a slight problem. Another smaller wood was located on the opposite side of the park. That also contained rabbits and provided an escape route. To overcome this problem, after long-netting the main wood two of us would walk behind the rabbits and set a net along the small wood. We called this back-netting. Of course in doing this we were inadvertently upwind of the rabbits then out to feed, and numbers would head for the main wood. We safeguarded ourselves by leaving one man behind to clear the rabbits that became entangled in front of the main wood.

I could never understand the logic of taking the doe rabbits away to warren systems. I felt sure lots of them would already have young to rear and by transporting the does elsewhere the young were doomed to die wastefully. I suppose it was possible that after being handled they would forsake their young anyway. The does were retained in hessian sacks and I have known some to bite a hole in the sack and escape. Sometimes when the demand for rabbits had become acute we were obliged to net when conditions were less than favourable, mostly when wind was non-existent. During July, August and September there would be quite heavy dew in the sheltered hollows along the wood. This made working conditions most unpleasant, the nets becoming wet and heavy to handle. When picking them up one's legs became wet.

There was the extra work of drying all the nets the following day, plus the repairs, the gutting and hanging of the rabbits and

A long-net is staked out horizontally to dry each morning after it has been used.

Repairs to the long-net. Some damage is inevitable.

the release of does in a warren. By the time the job was done, breakfast was certainly appreciated. Some of the nets in use were those I had made myself. Lots more were nets confiscated from poachers at various times, nets of all colours, lengths and mesh sizes. The diversity of material was due to the fact that much of it came courtesy of local mill-owners.

Rabbit netting was the main poaching preoccupation of that area and there was always a ready market for live rabbits to sell to miners for training their whippets, of which there were many. These confiscated nets were a very motley collection. Mesh sizes were often as small as 1¾ or 1½ inches (about 4 – 6 centimetres) from knot to knot – poachers' nets indeed, for nothing worthwhile could pass through. The material was often double-stranded to overcome its thinness, and was garish in appearance.

Their netting stakes were no more than 2 feet (60 centimetres) in length, to slip nicely into poachers' pockets for concealment. They were made from a variety of timber, some from sawn splines and with points burned to make them hard. They pegged their nets about every 5 yards (4·5 metres), pegging top to bottom lines. This was necessary because the nets were not very high and one rabbit caught midway between stakes would sag the net and allow other rabbits to escape over the top. The poachers used stones to frighten their rabbits into the net, walking about and rattling one against the other. If confronted by keepers they used the stones as missiles in their bid to escape. The only defence against this in total darkness was to remove your jacket and hold it in front of you with both hands as a shield. When the poachers ran out of stones the chase began. . . .

Many gangs were apprehended and their gear confiscated, most of it ending up in our possession. They were a generally unscrupulous lot. On one occasion I even recall a rearing field containing young pheasants being raided. The broody hens were taken and the young pheasants ignored. Robbed of warmth, all the young birds died.

I can recall an incident early one September when I had a net carried away on to a hedge. There were a number of rabbits in the net but I never believed that it was the sheer weight of the catch that was responsible. More likely the net was carried away because the ground was bone dry and hard and I hadn't been able to push the stakes deep enough into the soil. I netted the same ground six weeks later and had a very good kill of rabbits, but in the whole of my long-netting career I have never known a net to be genuinely swept away by the weight of the rabbits it caught. If a long-net is correctly set it should be capable of withstanding any weight of rabbits. I had no trouble the night I got 94 in one setting – although I have heard tales from other warreners who have suggested this has happened to them.

7

Organised Rabbit Shoots

Organised rough rabbit shoots, aimed at bagging those rabbits that either live permanently above the ground or may be temporarily induced to do so, takes place annually in the period from February to early April. By that time much of the ferreting will have been completed and the organised shoots are intended to clear up those rabbits that have proved very hard to get by all other methods. So the rough rabbit shoot is another of those highly sporting prospects with a purpose – and they are undertaken at the time of year when there are as yet very few young rabbits. All the rabbits, give or take a few, will be mature – and on the point of breeding and enlarging the stock. The vegetation is dormant. It has been laid low by frost and a winter's decay. The rabbits can be relatively easily flushed from the remaining cover.

Through the autumn and winter rabbits will have been killed by a variety of methods and many of those remaining will be thoroughly touchy and very easily disturbed. Those which the ferrets have failed to bolt or which have not been killed by other means will have learned the wisdom, from their point of view, of sitting tight and not budging. Those that have lived above ground have adapted to the terrain and have made themselves comfortable in situations from which they have not budged on previous occasions.

So by the time the rough rabbit shooting days arrive there are, in effect, two populations of rabbits to consider – those which were forced from burrows by ferreting and which now live on the surface and those which have so far resisted the ferrets' efforts and have remained underground. In fact, some of the rabbits that have been evicted from burrow systems will have moved on to other systems and will have even reinhabited emptied ones.

Forcing Rabbits above Ground

You can, of course, conduct rough shooting campaigns against the surface-living rabbits and kill some, but it figures that the effort is very much more worth while if you can force those rabbits living underground to emerge, if only for a few days, so that you can then further cream off both rabbit populations simultaneously. There are a number of ways in which rabbits can be forced from underground into open-ground situations. To do that the warren systems must be made uninhabitable, if only for that period.

So, over as short a period as can be managed while covering all the warren systems and burrows available to you, these are worked on to force the rabbits above ground. There are many methods that can be used to effect the purpose. Some people, those concerned solely with killing the rabbits regardless of the means, use gas at this time. This may seem extremely thorough and it is beyond doubt that gas is a killer – but if it is so effective it is right to wonder why after a burrow has been gassed rabbits often emerge from that burrow and escape to the surface. There is a failure in application. I think I know why this is, but from my point of view it is best unpublished since I am perfectly happy for the limitations of gassing to remain so that the sporting methods get greater emphasis.

One of the more popular methods of 'stinking out' burrow systems to make the holes uninhabitable is the use of newspaper soaked with paraffin. A ball of paper is dipped in paraffin and is then pushed with a stick as far down each hole as possible. All holes are treated bolt-holes and entrances alike. Each one is given its newspaper and paraffin treatment and each is then completely sealed with soil. The smell percolates through the entire underground system and the rabbits object and force their way out, making it obvious as they do so that they have left.

There are other stinking-out methods. Some people merely insert the newspaper and set light to it. This has a smoking-out effect of short duration only and is dependant on a draught forcing the smoke through the system. The smoke must be allowed to penetrate the complete underground system before the holes are blocked.

Small potatoes dipped in creosote and thrown into all

entrances and exits are another popular way. There was a time when I used a proprietary liquid called Renadine. A piece of sacking was tied to the end of a stick, dipped in the liquid and then thrust down each hole. One dipping was sufficient for several holes. The Renadine had a most pungent smell that persisted for several days; the rabbits loathed it and left home. This was very effective but if you accidentally spilled any on your clothes you would reek of it for weeks.

I have a method of my own which I consider hard to beat. It is labour-saving, cheap and quick. It involves first of all the collection and then drying of quantities of fir cones. It is a comparatively easy matter to collect these whenever you are in the right area, place them in a skip or container and let them dry thoroughly some weeks at least before they are needed. When required, they are dropped into a container of creosote and left to soak for a few minutes. They are then removed and drained off, which makes them easier to work with and allows the remaining creosote to be used again. Since they are lightweight, it is possible to carry a large number and I fill a 4-gallon (20-litre) plastic bucket with the treated cones (I put a rubber glove on my right hand) and I am ready to start. A cone is positioned in every entrance and exit. Because they are rounded in shape they can be delivered with an underarm action and will roll some distance down most holes, where they are then all the more effective.

Whichever stinking-out method of those described is employed the follow-up treatment is exactly the same. All holes, bolt or entrance, must be closed up – and this is time well spent. It figures, of course, that the bigger the area treated at the same time the better. The rabbits over a wide area have no alternative but to stay above the surface and find the available cover. Miss one or more holes and you provide a safe haven underground so it is very important to be extremely thorough in this work.

The ideal workforce is three people – one to position the fir cone and two to block up all the holes afterwards. It can be done single-handedly but this is time-consuming and more exhausting, for that one man is required to carry the cones and a spade over the entire area.

The stinking-out must be completed four or five days prior to the shooting effort. If the weather is dry the rabbits are much more likely to stay above ground, whereas if it is wet there is the

Fir cones soaked in creosote are rolled into each burrow entrance and the smell forces the rabbits to the surface.

prospect that some will attempt to get back below ground even though the burrows may be objectionable to them.

The Shoot

Try to plan well in advance. Fix your shooting day so that good guns are available to do the killing for you. You need reliable people, safe as well as capable shots. Any Tom, Dick or Harry won't do. Anyone can obtain a shotgun certificate but that doesn't make him or her either safe or proficient. Rabbit shooting is often snap shooting. You must have confidence not only in your own ability but in the prowess of others too. Beware of the man who may be likely to bring a friend on the day, someone who he will describe as a fellow who doesn't often get the chance of a shot but who would love to shoot some rabbits. He is the man who is most likely to violate the safety factors, put everyone else on edge, take the pleasure out of the day – and reduce the bag.

Since these rough rabbit days are both functional and pleasurable the guns invited to take part are usually a mix of those to whom the organiser owes some shooting and some fun and those who can do the job well. The tenant farmer is an obvious choice if he is interested enough to come along. He is then made aware that the shoot is organised in his interests, his crops will benefit if the rabbits are killed, and he is given joint responsibility for the kill. Thus, if he fails, the rabbits that survive are as much his responsibility as anyone else's. He had the chance and missed it and shares the blame when the resulting horde of young rabbits feeds on his land through the coming months.

The thickness of the cover and the width of the woods, belts, and strips to be worked decides the number of walking guns to be employed. In dense cover it may be necessary to have a man for every ten yards and to make haste very slowly. A most important point is that each gun makes a great contribution to his own shooting. He is his own beater. It is not enough merely to walk forward through the cover. It must be very carefully searched out, with each man treading on and into all grass, bramble and cover of any description to ensure that all the rabbits are moved out and forwards.

Early in any drive the walking guns are free to shoot at all rabbits that are disturbed. These can be shot whether running forwards or backwards in relation to the direction of the drive. Bearing in mind that a rabbit can show at any time, the walking guns must keep in line. Only then can they be completely sure that they have a clear line of shot. When walking guns straggle and some get out of touch, not only does the safety aspect become jeopardised but rabbits are then flushed much more indiscriminately and are more difficult to dispose of.

So every drive must progress at the speed of the slowest man – which doesn't mean the slowest is creating any delay. It is much more likely that the slowest at moving forwards is making the greatest contribution to the day's events by working all the cover in front of him and leaving nothing undisturbed. Everyone must remember that cover is not of identical density all the way across the line of walking guns. Men progressing through brambles are inevitably delayed, whereas those moving through more open land, grass and the like, tend to get ahead.

After the drive has progressed some distance it is often advisable to drop off two of the walking guns to take up position in the rear. It is inevitable that more rabbits will be flushed from thick cover and go back undetected and these can be picked off by the rear guns if sensibly positioned. In the meantime, the walking guns continue to move forward, shooting as they go until they are some 150 yards (135 metres) from the positions allocated to the numbers of standing guns that may be required to cover the full width of the walkers effectively.

When this point is reached the shoot organiser either blows a whistle or gives some other clearly audible signal to notify the guns. Then neither those walking nor standing may shoot forwards to threaten one another. Shooting continues with all guns then shooting behind, into the vacant areas where no one is in any danger. The walking guns continue to move forward, recognising that there are likely to be a number of rabbits concealed in the final part of the drive since these have been reluctant to attempt to escape through the standing guns. Every possible point of concealment is disturbed and the drive completed.

The standing guns will have been in position virtually from the time the drive first began. It is their task to deal with all the rabbits flushed forwards by the walkers. The line of standing guns is usually located in a clear area offering maximum but not complete visibility. For, while the guns themselves must have clear sight of the area both in front and behind them, it is also very important that they should be at least modestly concealed.

They must do a number of things. They must stand in line; each gun must know the exact position of his neighbours: and they must conceal themselves, standing still and keeping quiet. No talking, no fidgeting, no cups of coffee. Every gun must be on the ball, keeping constant vigil, for a rabbit can appear at any time. In fact, if the rabbits are unduly nervous some will almost inevitably show very early in the drive. The best rabbit shot, in my opinion, is the man who shoots his rabbits when they have passed him. That way there is not the slightest danger of harming anyone else.

On most occasions the walking guns may be accompanied by non-shooting beaters. These people can be given another duty. They carry the rabbits shot by the walking guns, allowing the

Rabbits are legged and hung up as soon as possible to cool.

guns to shoot again and as often as may be necessary, freed from the restriction of carrying rabbits they have already shot. The standing guns should leave the picking up of the rabbits they have killed until the drive has finished since more rabbits can come into range at any time.

Once the drive is completed all the rabbits that have been shot must be collected at a convenient point from which they can be picked up later. They should be legged immediately and hung head downward in exactly the same way as rabbits killed while ferreting.

Using Nets in Rough Shooting

Long-nets can be used in conjunction with rough rabbit shooting for a dual purpose. The nets can entangle rabbits in the normal way but they can also be used to subdivide large areas of very thick cover, thereby making it much easier for all the rabbits to be flushed forwards towards the waiting guns. Rabbits first emerging from thick cover or progressing through it generally move very slowly. They tend to hop from point to point rather than break into full speed – since they are in any case fairly well concealed. Therefore when these rabbits approach the net they may make contact with it but will simply brush against it and be diverted forwards. They are not travelling fast enough to become entangled.

If nets are used in this way the guns must be disciplined not to shoot towards or into the nets, for serious damage can and will follow, and the net will require extensive repairs. Square, otherwise unmanageable blocks of small, closely planted firs can be handled in this way. A wood of 60, 70 or even 100 acres can be divided in half by a wall of net set down the middle and then treated as two separate drives, without one half becoming confused with the other. Thus the rabbits can be systematically cleared from each half. Provided long-netting is available in quantity, even the very largest woods can be split into sections and dealt with a piece at a time.

There are some situations in which the walking guns are unable to shoot in any direction. The cover may be so dense and restrictive that they can neither see a bolting rabbit nor effectively put their gun up to shoot at it. In those situations they must continue to perform their beating duties since each man is to some extent dependent on the others for his sport. Provided the rabbits continue to be flushed forward there is no loss of potential in the drive. If the walkers stay in line the rabbits will be the more likely to move in the required direction, whereas if the line deteriorates into a disorganised rabble the rabbits will bolt in all directions.

The standing guns can also have problems. They may be positioned in a comparatively narrow ride or clearance within dense cover, such as small conifers. This can be the most testing shooting of all. The rabbits dart across quickly, often very close at hand, making fleeting and impossible targets. The pattern of shot doesn't spread enough to allow any margin for error; and, should you connect, the rabbit is so badly damaged that it will be worthless in marketing terms. I was once invited to shoot in such a spot in a 9- or 10-year-old conifer wood. It was some six acres in extent and was surrounded in its entirety with rabbit-proof netting. The netting had lost its effectiveness simply because of over-enthusiasm on the part of the farmer or his workmen. A

The scene during a rough rabbit shoot in conjunction with long-nets.

tractor had tried to plough too close to the netting, the inevitable happened and the wire was torn over long areas in a number of places . . . and not repaired. This created a natural habitat for the local rabbits since they were able to move into an area of quite dense cover, thick grass and bramble flourishing wherever the light penetrated to the ground. Not only was the cover thick but it was warm in there too – a perfect hiding place for large numbers of rabbits.

Our first step was to position a number of short long-nets, mainly only 20 yards (18 metres) in length, in front of all the holes in the wire netting. Then the four standing guns were positioned in the clearing which was some 150 yards (135 metres) long and not more than 5 yards (4·5 metres) wide. We took our places all facing along the clearing in the same direction. We stood on the side of the ride nearest to the approaching beaters. This enabled us to shoot what in other circumstances would have been each other's rabbits. I must make it clear that we were all highly experienced shots, all gamekeepers in fact, and we were able to do this without endangering each other. The rabbits were thus shot at greater range than could otherwise have been the case and we all benefited from the fact that we were looking in the same direction. We didn't turn around since the next gun was covering the area behind us. I can't recall the exact score but I believe we killed some 120 in that single drive. We could not have succeeded any other way.

We shot the same wood one week later and proved to our certain knowledge that we had very largely cleared the area since the second effort barely produced a score of rabbits. But it is quite rare for one roughing up to be as effective as that one proved to be. In normal circumstances the operation can be repeated in a week's time with the expectation that, all things being equal, the bag must be something rather less than 50 per cent of that obtained first time.

There are situations where it is almost impossible to position standing guns to shoot rabbits that are flushed forward. These are vast areas of open scrub land, areas of grass and heathland, and they are best shot by a long line of guns all walking forward. This allows everyone to shoot both backwards and forwards but, because of the vast tracts of land being walked, it is a slow process. There can be as much as 30 yards (27 metres) between the guns, there is much diagonal walking to be done and the movement forward is quite slow if the flushing is to be done efficiently.

There are some situations where large numbers of walkers, with or without guns, are unnecessary – hedgerows and small spinneys, for example. These are generally three-man operations, with the flushing work being done by dogs. When working hedges, one man walks each side while the third takes up position in the nearest gateway or clearing through the hedge to intercept rabbits bolted forwards. The necessity here is for a roomy sidebag since there is no one else to carry the rabbits – and your hands must be left free to allow you to use the gun.

One most important factor in respect of rough shooting is wind direction. Always walk rabbits down-wind if possible.

8

Night Shooting Techniques

Without question the most effective means of reducing rabbit populations fast is by night shooting with a ·22 rifle. Some very big bags indeed can be steadily accumulated after harvest through to the mid-April period of the following year. But this is very specialised work indeed. It is definitely not for the beginner nor for those who cannot shoot well. There are important safety factors which must be taken into account and because of the power of the weapon being used caution is the first necessity.

This is underlined by the fact that whereas almost anyone can obtain a shotgun licence – for those who are physically and mentally fit there is little problem – to use a ·22 rifle requires the owner to obtain a firearms certificate. This is a much more difficult licence to obtain. Everyone who makes an application is, in fact, vetted by the police, there is an inspection of the land on which the rifle is intended to be used and even when a licence has been granted the owner may be required to stipulate the exact areas in which it will be used. It follows, therefore, that night shooting with a rifle is not a sport for the beginner.

The terms under which a firearms certificate is issued tend to vary around the country. My own certificate defines the precise areas where I can use the weapon but in some other instances applicants get a more open certificate which authorises them to use their rifle wherever they have permission to do so. My certificate limits me to the purchase of only 1,000 rounds of ammunition at any one time and recommends, although it doesn't insist, that the rifle should be kept under lock and key at all time when not in use. This makes very good sense but it also underlines the point that a ·22 rifle is potentially lethal and must be treated accordingly.

Taking that into account, anyone wishing to take up rabbit

shooting after dark must first learn to use the rifle to a high standard during normal daylight hours. He must become proficient at handling the rifle as well as becoming an accurate shot – and at the beginner stage this can only be accomplished during daylight. Only once a man becomes totally capable with the weapon and can shoot well with it can he begin to think of using it after dark.

Choosing a Rifle

Never be in a hurry to buy a rifle. Have a good look around at the various possibilities. There are a variety of makes, shapes, weights and actions. Above all else you need a weapon you can grow to like and which will therefore give you the best possible results. It is important not to make a mistake for a second-hand rifle loses its value much faster than a second-hand shotgun. There is much-reduced demand for a rifle simply because a much smaller proportion of the population either wants one or is able to use it. My own weapon is a Remington 16-shot automatic I have owned for twenty years. I made up my mind that it was the rifle I needed, learned to use it and it has given me outstanding service – and will continue to do so. I am highly satisfied with it and see no reason to change or to spend more money on what some other people might regard as a better one. The best rifle for you is the one you can use best. It is probably true that virtually every rifle made today is a good one and it is simply a matter of determining your own preference and sticking with it.

So far as night shooting is concerned I believe that much of the secret of success is in the ammunition used. I prefer Winchester hollow-nosed subsonic bullets. These are more than adequate to my needs and have the added bonus of being quieter than the heavier loads. In any case, I think it makes sense from the safety viewpoint not to use high-velocity ammunition after dark, since the rabbits to be shot will generally be found within 80 yards (72 metres). Telescopic sights are essential for after-dark shooting. They are more accurate and they give the user a better sight of his target since he shoots with the aid of a light either from his vehicle or from a hand-held lamp.

It is important that you should know your land in great detail for every type of shooting. This is much more important when using a rifle. You must be aware of the location of all roads, all footpaths, all houses and all livestock – and you must cultivate the habit of never chancing a shot. Where there is even the slightest element of risk, never shoot. Better to wait, for sooner or later that half-chance will become a real and better chance some other time.

A ·22 rifle used for night shooting must have its sights adjusted for use at 40 yards (36 metres) range. It is relatively easy for an experienced shot to hit virtually every rabbit in the head at this range and if I miss with two consecutive shots my next shot is at some other target that happens to be available, not at a rabbit. For if I miss twice I am sure I must somehow have accidentally jarred the sights of the rifle within the vehicle. A ·22 needs to have its sights only fractionally out of alignment for the shot to miss. Time and ammunition expended on the occasional target shoot is never wasted. There are simple adjustment devices for elevation and horizontal correction on all 'scopes.

Night Shooting in Practice

Night shooting scores in exactly the same way as night netting in that it catches rabbits when they have left the security of their burrows to feed. Darkness appears to give the rabbits a false sense of security. They run neither so far nor so fast as they would when disturbed in daylight. The light being used to identify the target may help in this respect. It may partially dazzle and confuse the rabbits so that there is a greater tendency to sit tight.

The best nights are dark and dry with a slight breeze. I have always thought that a good netting night is also a good shooting night. When it is wet the rabbits do not leave their burrows for as long, neither do they travel so far as when ground conditions are dry. It is, though, nearly always possible to kill some rabbits almost regardless of the conditions. There will always be a few available but there are obvious advantages in going after them on the nights when the greatest numbers of rabbits are on the surface. If the wind is strong, though, this does create vibration on your vehicle which affects the accuracy of your shooting.

Night shooting has come a long way since its earliest days, when farmers used the lights from a moving tractor to spot the rabbits for a walking gun. The gun walked beside the tractor and shot the rabbits as they came into view in the tractor's headlights. In those days the weapon used was almost invariably a shotgun, but the ·22 rifle began its climb to prominence with the arrival of four-wheel-drive vehicles and the introduction of plug-in-type, improved-performance handlamps. These take their power from the vehicle, not from a dry battery, and the result is a constant power source and a much better light.

I much prefer to shoot from a Land Rover. I both drive and shoot, with an assistant holding the lamp out of the passenger-side window. He has the task of spotting targets at close range, simply holding the beam steady on the target once it comes into view. The rabbit is likely to stay still, giving me the time needed to shoot it. I am easily able to see rabbits that show within the lights of the Land Rover so the functions of the assistant is really to extend the width of the area being searched. If a long or a difficult shot is in prospect, I switch off the ignition and this helps by steadying the vehicle.

Rabbits must be picked up immediately after they have been

The firing position for after-dark shooting from a vehicle using a ·22 rifle.

The hand-held lamp backs up the vehicle's headlights when searching for rabbits in the night.

shot. To leave them lying where they were killed is to toy with fate, for there is no landmark in an open field after dark and your chance of returning to exactly the same spot to find the rabbit is very much a matter of luck. There is no point in chasing individual rabbits around and around a field. That only makes them all wild and flushes other rabbits and you then forfeit the chance of killing that night. Make haste slowly. Be methodical and if the chance comes to kill more than one rabbit at one stop do so, again working slowly and methodically and killing the rabbit that's furthest away first. But take great care to mark where the first one was killed, so far as this is possible, before turning to the second . . . and the third. I have killed as many as five rabbits before moving on to continue the search.

Rabbits will invariably run out of the field towards the bank, where their burrows are most likely to be situated, but it is very rare indeed for a rabbit to run headlong into the bank. Just before

146

disappearing from view it stops and presents the opportunity of a shot. I estimate that 75 per cent of all rabbits I have killed after dark with a rifle have been shot within a yard or so of the bank. This is perfect, for the bank presents a backstop for the bullet and it can go no further. In places where there is no bank, but where the field ends with a fence or with a wood or belt of trees, the rabbits are much more inclined to continue running straight ahead and out of sight.

The searching pattern in each field is to drive the Land Rover slowly around the headlands not more than 15 yards (13·5 metres) from the bank or fence, completing a full circuit of the field. My assistant is searching the land to the left of the Land Rover so that our joint efforts search through an area some 40 yards (36 metres) wide. If rabbits are evident I will repeat the search by driving round the same field a second time over the same line of search. Some rabbits will have travelled further out into the field from the hedge, will have been disturbed, and will have run some of the way back home.

Therefore a second sweep over the same ground establishes

An excellent night's work with a rifle, all gutted and ready for market.

contact with rabbits that were not in that area the first time round. The great advantage of this method of searching is that it does not disturb the whole field and those game birds which may be sleeping out in the middle of the field are left undisturbed. Later on, when the game-shooting season has ended, I feel no need for this restriction and will then search each field more thoroughly. In those areas where no consideration need be given to game birds (perhaps there are none) the search can always be thorough.

Night shooting has to end in the springtime when growing corn and vegetation is so high that the rabbits can no longer be seen. Squatting rabbits are generally located by the reflection of the car lights or the lamp in their eyes. It is important to be able to distinguish between one species and all the others, and you determine this when you look through your 'scope to assess the target. Then and only then can you tell for certain whether what you have seen is a rabbit or something else. Light reflects in the eyes of horses, cattle, cats, foxes, hares and some game birds so you must take great care when you weigh up the potential target.

One big advantage of using a ·22 rifle fitted with a silencer instead of a shotgun is that rabbits which are missed or not even seen at all are never scared. There is no noise. The rabbits are either undetected or they make their exit from the field, and since they have not been frightened in any way you can expect them to return to that same feeding ground quite quickly. Perhaps the same night – certainly the following night. So the silencer allows you to shoot over each field virtually night after night while conditions are favourable and reduce the rabbit population severely. You must, though, be mindful of the noise factor at all times. The Land Rover doors must never be slammed and talking is permissible only so long as it is quiet.

During wet weather, when the land softens, the weight of the Land Rover can do considerable damage to growing crops. To minimise this the vehicle should be driven along the tracks already made in the growing corn by the farm vehicles, fertiliser and spray machines that tend the crops from the moment when they are first sown. However, there are inevitably times when the soil is waterlogged and it becomes impractical if not impossible to take the Land Rover through gates and gaps where the terrain is likely to be especially sticky. In borderline cases four-wheel-drive Land Rovers and similar vehicles come into their own. Some soils, of course, are much more negotiable than others. On light sandy soil the effect of prolonged rainfall disappears very quickly as the result of better drainage, but heavy soil retains the water that much longer and prevents access for some days. If you are lucky enough to have a choice then clearly you work the land to suit conditions at the time.

It is important to take whatever advantage you can from the crop situation. For example, a field of sugar beet could provide dense cover for a number of rabbits which may have taken up residence there. You may well guess that some are in there but you haven't seen them previously. In any case you can do nothing while the beet remains unharvested. However, modern root crop harvesters work very quickly. A complete field of beet can disappear in a single day and the rabbits which were previously so well concealed have suddenly lost their home and cover.

They still feed there after dark, eating the remnants of the crop, but are otherwise sitting and hopping around in an apparent state of confusion. It is possible to actually witness this in the aimlessness of their movements. They are, therefore, comparatively easy targets until they have become accustomed to the new conditions. The lesson here is to shoot over the ground as quickly as land conditions allow you to get there.

The Three-Wheel Motor Cycle

A more recent development has been the increasing popularity of three-wheel motor cycles. My son-in-law, Andrew Seaman, a gamekeeper all his life, bought a Honda machine with tyres 9 inches (23 centimetres) wide but with a tyre pressure of a mere 2 lb per square inch (014 bar). This enables the bike to be taken on to the softest ground and over the most vulnerable of young crops without inflicting the slightest damage. The tyre marks are only very faintly visible. A machine of this type can also be used to cross low-lying marshes and is able to go where Land Rovers and other heavier vehicles would have no chance at all.

The model he uses is a Honda Big Red ATC, the ATC standing for 'All Terrain Cycle'. It is fitted with a 200cc engine, has an automatic clutch, weighs 3cwt (150 kg) and has a turning circle of just 10 feet (3 metres). The capacity of the fuel tank is sufficient for more than nine hours' continuous running time with the fuel consumption approximately a third of that of a Land Rover. It is a highly mobile machine with only one notable disadvantage – the width of the tyres makes it unsuitable for use on stubble. The stubble stalks are crushed and the subsequent noise given off frightens the rabbits so that they do not sit tight.

Since the tyre pressure is so low there is a high degree of wear on tarmac surfaces but the machines cannot be licensed for road use, and there is very little tyre wear on soft ground. To counteract the road use limitation, Andrew has built his own trailer. He tows the trailer containing the motor cycle by Land Rover to the area in which he intends to operate, works that over thoroughly, reloads the machine on the trailer – simple enough – and moves elsewhere. It is all so very easy.

The three-wheel motor cycle, extremely effective transport over crops. The wide, low-pressure tyres minimise damage to growing corn. A heavier vehicle would sink to the ground. Andrew Seaman demonstrates the firing position.

He has rigged an aluminium box behind the seat and this is positioned so that he can pick up a shot rabbit from the ground with one hand, without getting off the bike, and drop it directly into the box. When this container is full the contents are transferred to the Land Rover. Andrew makes use of the standard lights on the motor cycle and they are generally adequate for search-and-find situations and for shooting too. But in addition he has built in a powerful spotlight that acts as an emergency light should the existing system break down.

As a result, he has a highly mobile method of operation and can go night shooting on virtually every occasion he feels inclined. He has made a number of highly satisfactory bags at times when he could have done little or nothing while using a more conventional vehicle. It isn't all plus. Nothing ever is. On the three-wheel cycle he is closer to the ground than he would be in the Land Rover with the result that rabbits are not always so

A rabbit is quickly dropped into the specially made container and the hunt continues.

151

From time to time rabbits are off-loaded from bike to Land Rover and hung on rails to cool.

visible once the growing corn gets to a height of five inches or so. There is an obvious advantage in looking down into the corn from a greater height, and the Land Rover does score here.

Another minus factor with the cycle is the distinct lack of protection from wind, rain and frost. During the worst of the winter Andrew did suffer somewhat and to minimise this problem he designed a throttle glove which was fastened to the handlebars. He can thrust his right hand into this while using the machine and withdraw it quickly once a rabbit is spotted and he needs to use the rifle. The glove stays in place and is conveniently available when needed again. All in all Andrew is highly satisfied with the motor cycle's overall performance and with his own results while using it.

He uses a 5-shot bolt-action SSA ·22 rifle and Eley hollow-point subsonic bullets. The bolt action increases the safety factor since he doesn't load his rifle until he sees a rabbit within range. It takes no time at all to transfer one bullet from the magazine to the

Reloading in the dark.

breach and in the event of any type of accident while riding over bumpy ground, for example, the rifle is empty. In this respect his bolt-action rifle is better than my automatic for use on the motor cycle.

Since Andrew works from the motor cycle in conjunction with his Land Rover, he has been able to convert the back of his Land Rover into a mini-gamecart. A series of rails and hooks is suspended across the vehicle and from time to time Andrew transfers the contents of his motor cycle container to the Land Rover. The rabbits are all legged and hung up when the transfer takes place, never thrown down in a heap, and as a result they retain their quality and appearance and are all the more marketable for that.

9

The Efficient Use of Snares

Catching rabbits with snares is not recognised as a sporting method. The people involved undoubtedly get fun out of it but this is not a method either for the novice or for the amateur. It is first and last a professional method which is applied in areas where other methods cannot or will not work effectively enough to control the rabbit stock.

Snaring comes into its own after harvest and through early autumn, although it can be carried out all the year round. Like long-netting, it can be considered a dying art, no longer practised by large numbers of people as happened fifty years ago. There is perhaps less need for it since other methods have largely replaced it. But, as a professional warrener of umpteen years' experience, I am still certain that snaring can continue to be a worthwhile method in the right circumstances.

The amateur rabbiter isn't, it must be said, totally commited to rabbit elimination. He may not even be dedicated to a massive reduction of the stock. Provided he kills enough to justify his effort and keeps the landowner or his tenant happy – to ensure that he can come again another year – he has no need to strive to kill the last remnants of the stock. The professional has to take a very different attitude. He knows full well that any stock deficiency in rabbits is purely temporary. The rabbits will quite quickly replace their losses – and usually manage to do this almost annually. So the professional realises that he must make a positive commitment to a programme of planned extermination, while also recognising that this too will never achieve a wipe-out.

The art of snaring – and I do think it is an art – consists in setting the snare efficiently and in exactly the right place. An advantage is that snares can be set and reset during daylight.

They are positioned on the rabbits' route from their burrows to the feeding grounds and should be examined at first light daily when the catch is collected and the snares reset. It is therefore a method to be used in situations where you are not allowed on the land at night or if you prefer always to work in the daylight hours. Once the snares are set the rabbits, in effect, catch themselves.

Snares can be bought in any good gunshop, even from an ironmongers, as can the cords and the prickers, the specially made sticks by which the snares are set – though every gamekeeper I know makes his own prickers. Keepers also make their own pegs, the stakes with which the snares are fastened to the ground. I make all my own snares at about a twentieth of the price you would pay in a gunshop or wherever for a complete snare ready for setting. All I buy is the brass wire. Four thicknesses of red baler twine secure the snare to the stake.

Snares are not set indiscriminately over a large area. They must be very carefully located in the travel routes the rabbits always use when travelling from burrow to feeding ground and back again. So before snares are set it is necessary to scrutinise the ground with great care to identify the runs the rabbits use. Grassland is the best to work on, although snares can also be set on ploughed land and on stubble. They can also be set to catch rabbits in cover and in woodland but the snag is that snares are liable to catch game birds and this must be avoided. So the best ground is open ground.

My aim would always be to set a complete line of snares across the field, not deviating more than a yard either way from a completely straight line. There is method in this type of approach. The snares are then easy to find – no search is necessary. Count your snares as you set them and you will know the exact number to collect when you finish. The straight-line setting speeds the process and the rabbits can be collected more easily and are carried no further than absolutely necessary. This also makes it much easier to be certain that every run receives a snare.

A snare line should not be set close to a hedge. I always like to set my snares at least 50 yards (45 metres) from the hedge or from the rabbits' points of access into the field. When a rabbit emerges from cover it does so slowly; then it hops around quite delicately, assessing whether or not it is safe to go further, before making up its mind and travelling at speed along the run to its feeding ground. Therefore, if the snare is set close to the hedge, the rabbits are likely to be merely hopping around rather than running and the chances of their being caught are much reduced.

Rabbit runs are quite easy to see. The line of travel shows up instantly in grass and a sequence of these routes can be seen across every field where any number of rabbits are working. On close inspection of any run it will be seen that there is a regular sequence of what I call daps and jumps. By jumps I mean the points at which rabbits thrust from the ground during their runs and at which they will also occasionally stop. The dap is the point where the front feet do little more than just touch the ground. The dap site is much less worn than the jump site. It is important to be aware of this since it is crucial to know the difference between the two. For a rabbit habitually runs in such a way that its feet are placed in precisely the same spot almost every time it travels along its run. Anyone who sets snares must be aware of this for only then does he know that exact place where each snare should be positioned. It figures that where the rabbit's feet are on the ground you need only to set the snare at the precise height to catch it, so the snare is set directly over the top of the dap since that is the one position in which you can anticipate the height of rabbit's head from the ground. So find the daps, where the ground is less worn than at the jumps, and you are halfway towards snaring your rabbits.

The snares must be properly set to be effective. The height of the snare is the crucial factor. The bottom edge of the ring of wire making up the snare must be no less than 4 inches (10·2 centimetres) from the ground, and on a wet night this distance can be increased to 4½ inches (11·4 centimetres). This may seem extraordinarily high but you will soon prove that this is the most effective height. Far more snares are set too low than are set too high. All you need to do is to set the snare so that the rabbit's chin passes over the lower part of the snare. If the loop of wire is narrow then a far larger number of the rabbits are caught in front of their ears and these die quickly. However, if the loop is narrow the margin for error is greater. As my prime objective is to catch the rabbit I prefer to create a somewhat larger loop. Most of the rabbits will die quite quickly.

A rabbit run, showing the sequence of jumps and daps, the key to the effective location of the snare.

The snare is in position.

The retaining peg is firmly heeled in.

Carefully set at the exact height to catch a rabbit.

The generally applied rule-of-thumb measurement for the exact height at which a snare should be set has traditionally always been the width of a man's hand. In a fully grown adult that is likely to be 3½ inches (9 centimetres); for women and youngsters it will be less. Therefore the width of the hand is not a constant measurement and in any case I have never thought it enough.

The pricker is a ½-inch (1-centimetre) diameter, 8-inch (20-centimetre) long length of dried hazel, sharpened at one end for easy penetration into the ground. At the top end the stick is sawn for some half an inch with a hacksaw and then split to a depth of just over an inch (2·5 centimetres) so that the wire, when inserted into the split end of the stick, is held tightly in position. I like my snares to be set to work in a pear shape and I am able to impose sufficient tension into the wire so that in the event of the snare missing a rabbit the snare is lightly brushed aside and then springs back into place. It can then catch the same rabbit on its return journey or catch the next one to travel outwards along the same run.

Snare pegs are made from green elder which becomes tough as well as light once dry.

The correct way to carry a number of snares.

The securing stake, by which the snare is tethered and held securely to the ground, is some 10 or 12 inches (25 centimetres) long, the longer stake being necessary in instances where the ground is soft. The stake is shaped like a wooden tent peg so that it cannot be easily pulled out of the ground. My stakes are always made with green, freshly-cut elder, a wood which is easily worked with a sharp knife and which is stored and allowed to dry and harden only after the shaping has been completed. Some people use ash pegs, I know, but elder is both lighter and tougher when dry, so a big bundle of fifty or so snares weighs appreciably less and the work is that much easier.

Dark nights are far and away the most effective. I set my snares during the morning, tend them the following morning, leave them to work a second night and then move them to a new site. With this method there is again the big advantage of a cleanly killed, undamaged rabbit that is sure to get the best price.

10

Appearance, Price and the Table

We don't just kill rabbits for sport, we also kill them for the table – and with this in mind we must ensure that our rabbits remain in the best possible condition. That point is equally true whether we eat them ourselves, give them to friends or sell them to the local game dealer or butcher. A rabbit that has been neglected after being killed can never look as well as one more considerately treated, and this is reflected in both appearance and price.

Legging, Hanging and Storing

Those people who bundle their rabbits into sacks immediately they have been killed and then forget about them until the end of the day are damaging the product's appearance and saleability. Thrown together in this way, a number of rabbits will overheat, blood from one will foul another, they stiffen in out-of-shape postures, they become difficult to leg, urine runs from one to affect others, and when tipped out of the sack they are indeed a sorry assortment.

To get it right there is a sequence of events you stick to every time. First kill your rabbit, then, if ferreting, complete the work in that particular dead-end of the burrow. Next leg your rabbits and hang them up. Legging is a simple operation which ensures each rabbit can, in fact, be hung up. You need a sharp knife and you cut from the hock down towards the thigh between the sinew and the bone of a back leg, making the cut about an inch long. While this is done the rabbit is held by its foot and hangs downwards from the hand. Make the incision and then pass the foot of the rabbit's other back leg through the hole until the hock has passed through. This can be done either by holding the rabbit back or belly towards you, since this is a matter of personal preference. If you have lost your knife, there is an alternative method for making the hole. Use the bottom teeth of the rabbit's jaw. Simply open the rabbit's mouth and force the bottom teeth through the leg and press downwards to extend the cut. Be warned, it's easier with young bucks than with old ones – and easier still with a knife and less time-consuming. So don't forget your knife.

With legging completed, the next task is to de-urinate the rabbit. Pass the thumb down the lower part of the rabbit's abdomen and the fingers down the backbone at the same time, and with a gentle squeezing motion expel the urine. The rabbits are now ready to be hung up. They are hung up to enable them to cool sufficiently and so that the body stiffens in the correct shape. If they are left on the ground they can be a distraction to ferrets still working around the burrow. They should always be hung out of direct sunlight. When this is strong the heat of the sun on the rabbit's paunch, usually full of food, gives off a gas which bursts the stomach by combustion. If this happens then gutting becomes a very messy business and the rabbit's flesh can be tainted.

Take advantage of whatever happens to be available for hanging the rabbits. They can be hung over bushes, fences, trees, buildings, or specially prepared rails within your vehicle. If there is any danger of the rabbits becoming flyblown – as there will be in late summer and early autumn – they should be legged into batches of four or five, hung on a single string and enclosed within a hessian sack. Put the sack around the rabbits so that they are enclosed, gather the mouth of the sack near the rabbits' feet and tie it around the string on which the rabbits are suspended. Make sure that there is no hole in the sack and the rabbits are then safe from flies.

If the rabbits are to be retained for any length of time before disposal they should be placed in a cold store. Some game dealers or butchers will accept frozen rabbits. In my younger days, long before freezers were available in the way they are now, I had to find a way of keeping my rabbits fresh. My mother used to keep her fresh milk and butter down the well inside a bucket, probably some 40 feet (12 metres) below surface level.

Make use of whatever is available to allow the rabbits to cool.

That was a good idea for me. I hung my rabbits down the well too, but I had to hang them suspended above a galvanised bath to ensure that no blood dripped out into the water. The rabbits stayed cool and away from insects.

Another method used at that time was to dig a hole in the garden, lay the rabbits out on hessian sacks, put more sacks over the top and cover them with soil. That would double the length of time the rabbits could be retained before being disposed of.

When I was a professional and had enjoyed a good day, killing perhaps 40 or 50 rabbits, there was no way I wanted to carry the weight of the intestines home with me. So, when the catch was completed, I dug a hole, gutted all the rabbits into it, filled it in afterwards and had less weight to cope with.

Gutting

Gutting a rabbit is a very simple task. You need a sharp knife and my own preference is for one with a very sharp point. I hold the rabbit around its rib cage with my left hand, knife in the right

First make a shallow incision when gutting your rabbits.

Enlarge the incision with the fingers.

The intestines are withdrawn and pulled free by hand.

The clean, unstained end product.

hand, with my thumb along the blade and covering all the blade with the exception of about an eighth of an inch. This protrudes just beyond the side of my thumb and is the controlling factor. It effectively limits the cutting depth and ensures that when the knife is drawn down the rabbit to about 3 inches (7·6 centimetres) below the rib cage only the skin and stomach lining are cut.

The art of gutting is to minimise the mess, to avoid contaminating your fingers unnecessarily and, of maximum importance, to avoid rupturing the rabbit's intestines. I insert the forefinger and thumb of my right hand and feel the paunch, which is located just below the liver. I then pull the paunch downwards, at the same time putting my other fingers underneath the main gut section, which enables me to lift the whole gut out in a single movement, leaving the liver behind. I would not deny that there is a knack. I had to do that job efficiently because I had to do it so often. Practice makes perfect and you may need a little practice before you can do it as well as you would like. Nevertheless, it is easy once you follow the correct sequence.

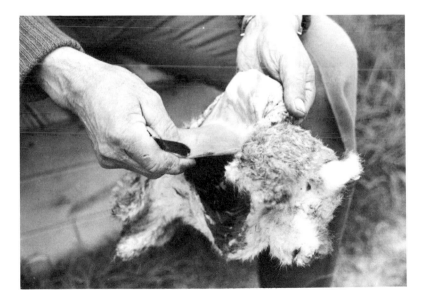

To skin a rabbit, first part skin from flesh at the gutting hole.

Above *Separate on both flanks to create a gap between back and skin.*

Right *The skin is removed from the back legs. Now cut off the tail.*

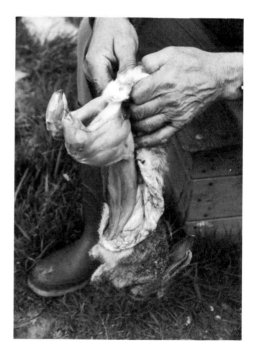

Above *Hold by the back legs and stretch the skin towards the head.*

Left *Remove front legs from the skin and the job is completed.*

Transporting Rabbits

Both before and after the rabbits are gutted, they have to be carried from place to place. As you progress through the day's work the number will hopefully mount up and you need a simple way of minimising the stress and strain of moving rabbits, tools, ferrets and all other impedimenta from site to site. To ensure that the rabbits can be conveyed easily, while leaving your hands free to carry such items as spades, guns and nets, there is a simple way. I can carry as many as thirty rabbits at a time without having one in my hand.

The method is to thread them on a 4-foot (1·3-metre) length of strong cord. Attach the first rabbit to one end of the cord and thread as many rabbits onto the cord as you think you can manage, simply passing the cord between their legs, and then fasten the last rabbit to the other end of the cord. Lay them out along the ground and take hold of the line some six rabbits away from either end, pick them up and with a swinging action throw them on your back. You will have six rabbits hanging in front of one shoulder and six in front of the other. The remainder will be hanging down your back.

To carry a number of rabbits, first thread a line between their back legs.

When slung over the shoulders, the rabbits are dispersed around the body, leaving the hands free.

One way, but not the best way, to carry rabbits.

This is just one example of how it can be done. With fewer rabbits you have fewer at the front as well as at the back, but strike a balance and the weight will be evenly distributed and you will find them quite easy to carry. The most important thing is that your hands remain free to carry other things, and this minimises the amount of to-ing and fro-ing required from site to site. Obviously, there is some blood but appearances are of little importance on a rabbiting expedition. You can wear your worst clothes – no one should wear anything better.

Nowadays most rabbiting expeditions involve the use of a vehicle of some description. It is therefore essential to get your transport as close to the scene of operations as possible, to minimise the donkey-work. I have seen many rabbits carried on a long spade or stick. This is very hard on the shoulders, which bear all the weight, and if you are walking on uneven ground the load swings to and fro and you become unbalanced. This method also occupies your hands and means that you cannot carry other gear at the same time. When hanging rabbits on a rail – in a shed, game larder or Land Rover – it is a good idea to hang them in couples, back to back. This means passing the hind legs of one rabbit through the hind legs of another. In this way they hang with their bellies facing outwards and air can circulate, keeping the rabbits in better condition.

Disposing of the Rabbits

Long before the rabbiting expedition you need to have some idea what you propose to do with the bag. No doubt you have friends. You also probably have a freezer, which may accommodate a limited number.

You may also see the rabbits as a source of revenue. So where, when and how do you sell them? And for how much? Game dealers and butchers are obvious outlets for any surplus. The professional warrener, who deals with large numbers of rabbits regularly, undoubtedly secures an ongoing contract with one or more outlets. The amateur's surplus will be less frequent and less predictable. He is unlikely to secure quite the same price as the professional – since he is less reliable. The price fluctuates according to demand, as does everything else. During the course of a full year it can be expected that the wholesale price of good-quality rabbits will vary up to 150 per cent.

During late summer and autumn there is a proportion of small rabbits in the kill and you cannot expect top price for these. So, in fairness to both the supplier and retailer, a price is usually fixed at such and such per pound. Thus you get a normal price for a big one and less for a small rabbit. When dealing in substantial numbers a game dealer buys by weight. You get so much per pound for the entire consignment.

A more recent development has been an increasing demand for rabbits to be sold with guts intact. These rabbits undoubtedly go for animal feed exclusively. Stomach content, after all, is merely fatty tissue and roughage, and all looks the same once processed.

A fly-proof game larder is the ideal temporary store before the rabbits are taken to the dealer. Only professionals and gamekeepers have that sort of facility available. The amateur must take advantage of the coolest, safest store he has available – and ensure that he keeps his rabbits there for no longer than is absolutely necessary.

For some years large shipments of frozen Chinese rabbits have been imported into Britain. This confirms that there is a big demand for rabbit meat, contrary to what some might have us believe. Much of this trade is as food for domestic pets but there is also another demand by hotels and caterers. These rabbits average 2 lb (1 kg) in weight each and are all of such similar size that they must be farmed rabbits, produced specially for market here and no doubt in other countries too.

The price at which the retailer must sell these rabbits makes a nonsense of the price paid in this country to warreners, gamekeepers and amateurs alike. A 2 lb (1 kg) British rabbit would be regarded as a small one. The Chinese rabbit averages only 2 lb (1 kg) yet the price difference is remarkable. The Chinese rabbit retails at double the price of its British counterpart.

There is a similar lack of logic in the comparative prices of tame and wild British rabbits. Who would dispute that the flesh of the wild creature, conditioned by a wide choice of food, is superior to that of the captive farmed animal? Yet the same remarkable price difference applies.

Skinning Your Rabbit

Whereas the rabbits you sell to game dealers and butchers are disposed of unskinned, if you intend to eat one or more yourself you must first remove its skin. This is another quite simple operation. I know, I can skin a rabbit in one minute. It may take the amateur a little longer but proficiency can be achieved quite quickly.

The first task is to remove the feet. These should be chopped off above the knuckle joint on a block. With a sharp knife, extend the gutting hole downwards to the full length as far as the vent. Now part the skin from the flesh on the edge of the gutting hole. Do this, one flank at a time, using both thumbs and forefingers. Skin and flesh come apart very easily under modest pressure. Continue the separation until you reach the backbone. Do this on both flanks until there is a gap between skin and rabbit. The next phase sees you pull the two back legs, one at a time, through the skin, leaving the skin attached to the rabbit at that end only by the tail. Cut the tail off with your knife.

Now hold the rabbit by the middle of its back with the right hand and pull the skin over its head with the left, using a stretching action. All that's left is to extricate the front legs in the same way as the back ones, and give the skin another pull so that it peels away as far as the neck. If you don't want the head you have skinned the rabbit. Cut off its head at the neck. Years ago we used to eat the head as well – there was some good flesh on it – but this is not general practice today.

Once all the skin is removed, cut through the pelvis and remove the small piece of intestine that remained after gutting and also remove the vent. If you intend to eat it, remove the liver. Carefully remove the gall bladder from the liver, making sure that you do not break the gall bladder. If you do you will make the liver taste very bitter.

Break the rib cage lining, put your hand up towards the neck and pull the heart out. Cut the heart off if you intend to cook it. It only remains to joint the carcase to your own requirements and, after washing it, to immerse it in salt and water overnight.

11

Favourite Dishes

Mrs Smithson's Rabbit Pie
For six people

Soak two mature rabbits in salt and water overnight. After cleaning, they should have been jointed into eight legs and four pieces of back. Dip in flour seasoned with salt and pepper to taste. Place in a large saucepan and cover with cold water. Bring to boil and simmer until tender, from 1¼ to 2 hours, depending on the rabbits (young rabbits will need less cooking, older ones more).

Once cooked, place in a pie dish, adding enough of the liquid to half cover the rabbit portions. Cut 4 oz (110 g) streaky bacon into rashers 2 inches (5 centimetres) long and lay them over the top of the rabbit.

Make sufficient plain pastry to completely cover the top of the pie dish with a crust ¼ inch thick (or as you like it). I don't use a pie funnel since the rabbit portions are high enough from the bottom of the dish to keep the pastry above the liquid. Beat one egg or, if you prefer, use milk and lightly brush over the top of the pastry to ensure an attractive-looking crust.

Place the dish in a hot oven and cook until the pastry is brown at an oven temperature of 375° F (190° C). Cook for 30 – 45 minutes. The pie is then ready to serve if you intend to eat it hot.

If the pie is eaten cold the gravy will have set into a white jelly. My preference has always been to eat cold with bread and butter.

Mother's Crock Pot Stew

To prepare my mother's favourite rabbit dish, first joint two rabbits and then immerse them in an earthenware stew jar which

173

also contains 8 oz (225 g) of sliced carrots and two large, sliced onions.

The jar is filled with liquid and the lid put into place. The jar is then placed in the cooking range oven and slowly cooked for two hours by the heat from a coal-burning stove.

When cooked, cornflour and pepper is mixed with water into a paste. A taste of gravy salt is included. Mother always used Burdalls gravy salt and so do I.

Stir the paste into the stewpot to thicken the gravy and provide extra flavour. Reintroduce the stewpot to the oven and reheat to boiling point. The rabbit stew is then ready to serve with vegetables of your choice.

Fried Rabbit

A meal of top quality requires four young rabbits, preferably less than half grown. These are jointed and immersed in salt water overnight.

Remove and dry them with a cloth. Dip them in ordinary flour and immerse in hot fat or oil, either in a frying pan or a deep fryer. Fry until golden brown, approximately 15 – 20 minutes, when the portions will be ready to serve hot with fried potatoes.

This is plain cooking but it preserves the flavour of the rabbit. You can use spices to choice but in our view this simply distorts the flavour of the meat.

Roast Rabbit

A very tasty alternative is to roast a mature young rabbit. After jointing, it is placed round a joint of pork within a roasting tin.

During cooking the fat from the pork compliments the rabbit and the flavour from the rabbit enhances the pork to improve the quality of both. Serve together, hot or cold, with vegetables of your choice. Cook for 20 minutes for each pound of pork, plus 20 minutes.

Index